Winds of Change

THE SOCIETY OF WOMEN WRITERS WA

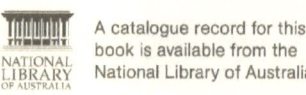

A catalogue record for this
book is available from the
National Library of Australia

Linellen Press
265 Boomerang Road
Oldbury, Western Australia
www.linellenpress.com.au

Dedication

To the courageous and creative women of the Society of Women Writers WA, whose words and imaginations resonate within these pages. Your stories and poems are not just words; they inspire, uplift, and challenge the world around us to think.

Contents

Dedication iii

Women Who Changed the World Jan Altmann 1

2nd July 1971 to 5th July 1971 Linda Blackshaw 8

No Signs or Symbols, Please Linda Blackshaw 12

All Our Yesterdays Maria Bonar 15

Bush Romance Villanelle Maria Bonar 16

Flame Tree Maria Bonar 17

Found Maria Bonar 18

Making Hay Sestina Maria Bonar 19

Moonlight Ghazal Maria Bonar 21

One Hundred and Two Maria Bonar 22

Quick Exit Maria Bonar 24

Waiting Maria Bonar 26

Western Front Maria Bonar 28

Meh! Erica Bowman 29

Stuck Erica Bowman 30

Across Two Worlds Aileen Boyer 31

Djeran Aileen Boyer 32

Fall Gal	Aileen Boyer	33
Out with the Old and In with the New	Aileen Boyer	34
A Future With AI	Lynne Cairns	35
Moon Madness	Lynne Cairns	37
People Like Us	Lynne Cairns	38
Super Comeback	Lynne Cairns	41
March Planting	Lynne Cairns	43
New Beginnings (Part 2)	Pat Curtis	44
Day One	Ros Day	47
Mavis – My Gift to Me	Lynne Doyle	57
Waiting	June Earle	61
The Watcher in The Mall	June Earle	64
Station to Suburbia	Raelene Hall	66
When Change is Forgotten	Caroline Hayward	68
Changing Friendships	Lynne Hunt	71
Changing Places	Lynne Hunt	79
Twin Hearts	Liz Hurst	85
A New Chapter in My Life	Melanie Hawkes	88
The Stick that Changed my Life	Melanie Hawkes	97
A Brand New Light	Helen Iles	101

A Change of Heart	Helen Iles	103
At Season's Break	Helen Iles	107
Stand Up	Helen Iles	109
Who's Coming to Tea?	Jean Alice Jenkins	111
Time to Say Goodbye	Dale Kerferd	119
Trinket Exchange	Kathleen Knight	127
A Dinosaur Called Therosorus	Nada Lubay	129
Checklist	Nada Lubay	139
Switch	Amanda Perlinski	144
More Than Meets The Eye	Marilyn Rainier	157
Duped	Shirley Rowland	165
Ghost Writer	Shirley Rowland	171
Song of Age	Shirley Rowland	174
With the Flick of a Switch	Molly Smith	176
I am Woman	Wendy Stackhouse	178
The Academy	Wendy Stackhouse	180
The Woods	Wendy Stackhouse	183
A Brother-Shaped Hole	Moira Yeldon	185
About The Society of Women Writers WA		190

Women Who Changed the World

Somewhere around 300BC, the great Aristotle declared that men had more teeth than women; therefore, women were incomplete or mutilated men! Because of such deficiencies, they did not have the 'manly virtues' of wisdom and rationality. It followed that the male was by nature superior and the female inferior, "the male ruler and the female subject". It followed also that women were not worth listening to, and so they were not permitted to participate in public debate. The struggle for women's rights is, more than anything else, a struggle to break out of this imposed silence – to be heard; and in making themselves heard, they expressed many new ideas, some of which even changed how human beings saw their world.

Perhaps Aristotle had not heard of a remarkable Athenian woman who had lived a few years before him. Aspasia of Meletus challenged the ideas of her time regarding the place of women in society. As the consort of the great general Pericles, Aspasia participated in public debates and helped him to write many of his politically charged speeches. In so doing, she demonstrated that women could be as intellectually capable, skilled in rhetoric and culturally influential as men.

Another brilliant and courageous woman who lived in these far-off times and who insisted on using her voice to challenge injustice and inequality was Hortensia. In 42BC, the Roman Senate proposed to raise money for the war against the assassins of Julius Caesar by taxing the property of 1,400 wealthy women. Hortensia was chosen by these women to confront the senators.

She agreed, and risking arrest and even execution, she pushed past the guards and delivered a powerful oration in the Roman Forum. She rebuked the senators for proposing to tax women to support wars that they had no say in. She declared that women would help to resist a foreign enemy but would never pay for civil wars. The speech angered the senators, but they did not have Hortensia dragged away and thrown to the lions. They reduced the number of women liable for the tax and imposed a similar levy on men. This meant that women were never again allowed to enter the Roman Forum.

Other women were ignored or even punished for speaking out. There was Hypatia, a teacher and thinker in ancient Alexandria around 470AD, who made significant contributions to mathematics, science and philosophy. She invented an instrument called the astrolabe, or 'star-tracker'. This was an ancient GPS that enabled people to use the planets for navigation and astronomy. It meant that these planets were no longer distant deities playing games with human lives. It gave them an entirely new way of engaging with the world around them. Unfortunately, Hypatia's Platonic ideas were seen as pagan and, as such, a threat to the Christian elite, which was in control at the time. She was dragged through the streets and murdered by a savage mob – her brilliance silenced for hundreds of years.

Women of the Middle Ages were usually wives and mothers, servants or nuns. Some were artisans, but few were able to express their own ideas. One outstanding exception was Hildegard of Bingam (1098-1179). Hildegard was a true polymath – a term usually only applied to male geniuses such as Leonardo da Vinci. She was a nun with many skills. She wrote poetry, treatises on theology and natural science. She also wrote music and practised healing. To have her writings accepted by the Vatican, however, she enlisted the help of a male colleague, and when they were accepted, they were attributed to 'the fathers of the church'. Hildegard did not receive due recognition until 1,000 years after her death.

Christine de Pizan of France. Born in 1364, Christine lost both her father and her husband when she was only 25 years old. She had three children and an elderly mother to care for, so she began offering her services as a writer. As far as we know, she was the first professional woman writer.

She began writing about women's issues because she could not find a book on morals that did not attack women with 'wicked insults'. In response, Christine wrote *The Book of the City of Ladies*. In this, she related a vision of three women – Lady Reason, Lady Rectitude and Lady Justice, who help her to build a city to defend women against baseless attacks. The Three Virtues populate their allegorical city with hundreds of women, historical and mythological, whose deeds provide evidence to counter their male detractors. As they build their city, the women take on everyone from Ovid to the guy who said, "God made women to weep, and sew." Lady Reason takes Christine to a Field of Letters, a fertile plain where she can use her voice and her pen to lay the foundations of this female society.

At the same time that Hildegard and Christine were speaking and writing, the first universities were being established, but of course, women were not allowed to attend. There was no specific rule barring women from universities, simply an assumption that the purpose of higher education was to prepare men for careers in the church or professions such as law and medicine. None of these was open to women. This is probably why, during the Renaissance, there were great male scientists like Copernicus and Galileo, but no female equivalents.

Despite this, some brilliant women were able to contribute to the momentous changes brought about by the scientific revolution of the seventeen hundreds. Émilie, Marquise du

Châtelet (1706-1749), a French mathematician and physicist, translated Newton's Principia Mathematica from Latin into French. Her explanation of Newton's law of gravity and his use of calculus made it clear that this Law applied equally to everything in Nature, including people. It raised questions as to why human laws should not also be applied equally to all people, and so it led indirectly to the fundamental changes brought about by The French Revolution.

During this time, the revolutionaries published *The Declaration of the Rights of Man*. One woman dared to respond to this by publishing a pamphlet entitled *The Declaration of the Rights of Citizens and Women*. For this, Olympe de Gouges was arrested and sent to the guillotine for 'forgetting her place as a woman.'

In 1787, in England, Mary Wollstonecraft wrote *A Vindication of the Rights of Woman*. In this, she argued that women were not naturally inferior to men but were seen as such because they lacked education. Inferiority was a social construct. Wollstonecraft argued that social norms caused women to be treated as witches or monsters. This was a passionate plea for equal rights and opportunities. Her detractors described her as a 'philosophical wanton' and 'a hyena in petticoats'.

The idea of femininity as a social construct was developed by Simone de Beauvoir, who firmly stated, 'One is not born, but rather becomes, a woman'. No biological or psychological fate determines the way that the human female presents in society; it is civilisation that produces this creature, intermediate between male and eunuch, which is described as feminine.

Opposed to femininity as a social construct was Carl Jung, one of the great thinkers of the twentieth century. He saw femininity as a natural attribute, which could be damaged by pursuits that were not 'feminine'. He wrote that 'by taking up a masculine profession, studying and working like a man, a woman develops a kind of rigid intellectuality that ends in neurosis.'

Despite this, many more women continued to change the world through their scientific discoveries.

Augusta Ada King, Countess of Lovelace (1815–1852), was the only legitimate child of the poet Lord Byron and his wife Anne Isabella Milbanke. Ada is known for her work on Charles Babbage's mechanical computer, the Analytical Engine. Her notes on the engine include what is now recognised as the first algorithm to be carried out by a machine. She is often described as the world's first computer programmer. She also developed a vision for computers to go beyond mere calculating, while others, including Babbage himself, focused only on those capabilities. Ada's mindset of "poetical science" led her to ask basic questions about how individuals and society relate to technology. It also led to what became the computer revolution of our own times.

In 1869, John Stuart Mill published a small but momentous work entitled *The Subjection of Women*. In this, he argued that 'the legal subordination of one sex to another is in itself wrong' and that it should be replaced by equality. In forming and publishing this pronouncement, Mill collaborated with his wife, the extraordinary Harriet Taylor Mill. They declared that there is not 'a shadow of justification' for not admitting women to the suffrage; and they followed this with the simple but powerful argument that there can be no democracy if half of the adult population is not permitted to vote.

This demonstrated a profound and fundamental change in thinking and reinforced Stuart Mill's idea that no great improvements are possible until a change takes place in models of thought (Autobiography 1873). There still a strong psychological resistance to change; however, this is mainly because it brings uncertainty, and uncertainty brings fear, anxiety, and resistance, especially when it comes to recognising the achievements of women.

One such achievement was the discovery of radioactivity. In 1903, the Royal Swedish Academy of Sciences awarded Pierre Curie, Marie Curie, and Henri Becquerel the Nobel Prize in Physics, "in recognition of the extraordinary services they have rendered by their joint researches on the radiation phenomena". At first, the Committee intended to honour only Pierre Curie and Becquerel, but one of its members and an advocate of women scientists alerted the others to the injustice of the situation, and after his complaint, Marie's name was added to the nomination.

In 1906, Pierre was killed in a road accident. Marie was devastated but continued her research. At first, the University of Paris refused to offer her a position, but relented and appointed her to the chair that had been created for Pierre. She accepted it, hoping to create a world-class laboratory as a tribute to him. She became the first woman professor at the University of Paris and the first woman to win a Nobel Prize. She went on to win another and to be the first to receive a Nobel Prize in two separate disciplines – chemistry and physics. Despite this, she was not admitted to The French Academy of Sciences, even though her discovery of radiation enabled X-ray machines to be taken into field hospitals on battlefields and eventually changed medical practice completely and forever after.

Florence Nightingale (1820-1910) not only gave nursing its professional status and revolutionised hospital care but also exhibited a gift for mathematics. She became a pioneer in the visual presentation of information and statistical graphics. She used methods such as the pie chart and her Rose Diagram, which she claimed even politicians could understand. Nightingale was elected the first female member of the Royal Statistical Society and later became an honorary member of the American Statistical Association.

In recent times, our knowledge of DNA has changed everything from diagnosing diseases to solving crimes. In 1962, the Nobel Prize for their discovery was awarded to James Watson and Francis Crick. A third member of the research team was ignored. Rosalin Franklin, an English biophysicist and X-ray crystallographer was the one who actually discovered the double helix, twisting ladder shape of its basic structure. Crick and Watson employed her research without her knowledge or permission. She died at the age of 37 and has become known as the 'dark lady of DNA.'

Another 'dark lady' of science is Vera Rubin, who studied the galaxy rotation problem and discovered dark matter. Although initially met with scepticism, Rubin's results were eventually confirmed. Her legacy was described by *The New York Times* as "ushering in a Copernican-scale change" in cosmological theory. It now seems certain that women will continue such changes.

Jan Altmann

2ⁿᵈ July 1971 to 5ᵗʰ July 1971

Damp Friday, throwing off the workday, settling in with a book. Those words could have been the beginning of a song, its background music the ringing of the telephone.

"Linda, Jenifer," my father yelled from downstairs.

Clambering downstairs, landing with a thump (I always jumped the last two) I picked up the phone.

"What d'ya want?"

"What are you up to?"

"Jenifer, what do you want? Thought you had plans."

"They changed. I want to go to the White Elephant tonight."

There went my plans. Curling up in bed reading a book would not cut it as an excuse.

"So?"

"You know Mum won't let me go without you?"

For some unknown reason, Jenifer's mother thought I was a good influence on Jenifer. I don't think I've ever been a good or bad influence on anyone. I was shy, BUT my one friend power was a refusal to do anything I didn't want to do. Only my stepmother thought I was a pushover, easily led. My friends could have told her differently. But, I digress.

"Don't want to."

"I'm meeting Andrew there?"

"I thought his name was John?" (I can't remember now, but I knew it wasn't Andrew.)

Jenifer let out a gusty sigh. "Linda, it doesn't matter. I want to go to the White Elephant. And you NEED TO COME

TOO." Jenifer's shout was a whisper. A whispered confession followed. "I've already told Mum you're going. So if you don't come, I can't go. I'll have to tell her you've changed your mind. YOU HAVE TO!"

That phone call on Friday, 2nd July 1971, changed everything. Because, of course, as a good friend, I changed my mind and we went out.

Nine pm, Jenifer and I rocked up to the venue. We lined up outside the Chinese restaurant, waiting to go through the door at the side. In dim lighting, we trudged up the stairs to the top floor. Once started, you had to keep going. The people at the top had to wait until the down was clear. Not enough room to pass each other on those stairs. Disco music echoed through the stairwell as a crowd of teens filed up the narrow climb to the discotheque.

When I took my jacket off and placed it on the chair back, Jennifer poked me. "What were you thinking?"

"What d'ya mean?"

She nodded downwards. I glanced down at my top and winced. It was white, all white. Nothing wrong with it. Except … in the strobe lighting, when all other lights went out, white gleams like a lighthouse lamp. I had forgotten about the ultraviolet light. Talk about standing out in a crowd.

In the 70s, I don't remember cocktails being a thing. My tipple of choice was a Bacardi and Coke. A few sips and the music took hold.

Now, I want you to close your eyes and visualise the scene. It's dark with the strobe lights flashing, and on one wall, cartoons play along with the music. The dance floor is full of bodies, shaking and gyrating in time to the music. Later in the evening, we will even do the twist. A few drinks later, a tap on my shoulder and a whisper in my ear. "Would you like to dance?"

I nodded. We exchanged names.

"Jimmy."

"Linda."

Then he asked, "Would you like a cigarette?" I declined, and he replied, "You could stick it behind your ear for later."

I laughed, and then the music stopped; a loud voice came over the loudspeaker. "The bar is closed. Any drinks left on the table will be removed in fifteen minutes."

"I have to go back to my table. I've a Bacardi to finish."

"Can I come with you. I've drunk all my beer." And I think he said, "I'll watch you drink."

As we drank, we chatted, and then the music increased in volume. He held out his hand. "Dance?"

To the strains of Rod Stewart and Maggie May, we shook and bumped shoulders and bums, then screamed along with Rod.

Then it was time to go.

I had a date to meet Jimmy at 5.30 pm the next night in George Square in Glasgow, just down from Queen Street Station.

Saturday, 3rd July

I went to a wedding that afternoon, so I turned up for my date wearing a turquoise and white hot pants suit. The top had a half-skirt attached that fell to mid-knee. A friend stayed with me as she said everyone knew that George Square was well known for people being stood up. I didn't mind passing the time with Liz as we talked about how lovely Christine had looked when she married Sam.

Also, I could not remember what Jimmy looked like. Luckily, as soon as I saw him walking up, I recognised him.

Liz took off before he reached us. Jim had brown, collar-length hair, was clean-shaven, and wore square, dark-rimmed glasses. He was five foot ten inches to my five foot one, and a bit, inch. Being smaller than I'd liked, I always threw in that bit.

We walked down to a Reo Stakis Steak House (can't remember its name). Jim ordered a salad, and mine was gammon steak. He said he wasn't hungry but wolfed down the salad anyway. We chatted about our surroundings unnoticed, until three firemen charged past our table, axes dangling off their belts. That is when we realised the room was full of smoke. We did not pay for our meals because the chef set the kitchen on fire. A lucky accident for us.

Jimmy confessed he only ordered the salad because he couldn't afford two meals. This was an era when if a boy asked a girl out on a date he paid – once they got to know each other, they used to take turns paying. And that was what Jimmy and I did in the future.

This was a memorable first date. On the Sunday, plans changed at the last minute, and we spent the afternoon in a park, walking and talking, getting to know each other. I discovered he taught himself to play the guitar. He played some Beatles and songs and music from the Humblebees, who were Billy Connelly and Gerry Rafferty, before they went their separate ways and found fame.

I can't remember all we talked about. We both listened to Radio Caroline, a pirate radio station that broadcast from a boat on the North Sea. And belted out Maggie May. We both read a lot and went to movies.

Monday 5th July

I told Jenifer Jim was the one for me. I let Jimmy discover that for himself, and we married on December 2nd 1972, one year and five months after we met.

Linda Blackshaw

No Signs or Symbols, Please

Some faceless people that no-one knows,
say a feather found is a sign that an angel is nearby,
or your dead father or mother
or a husband.
A feather signifies a message.
Or pennies or five cent coins.
The dead are thinking of you. So 'they' say.
What do I care? Sometimes, a feather is just a feather.
If a feather means you are near. I'd rather feel
your lips pressing mine or the touch of your hand.
Not a scent, I can't remember that any more
But I'm sure I'd recognise your energy
As you brush up against me.
I don't know; I haven't felt you close,
Except in dreams and memories.
Doves, butterflies or balloons are released
Not sure why, maybe symbolic of setting the soul free
Or carrying it to heaven. Save the doves.
save the butterflies and save the planet.
What has special meaning?
Our three children and music.
I can still hear you inside my head
Playing guitar and singing an Eric Bogle song or,
playing Scottish reels and Irish jigs or
a lament from Skye on your fiddle.

Not long after you died,
I saw a contest in the local paper.
WIN two tickets to the Nannup folk festival.
You'd have liked that.
Then I saw Eric Bogle was performing.
As I tapped in my name.
I said out loud, this is mine.
It was.
At his concert, I was happy/sad
I hoped you were there…ticket not required.
Often you see the question, which famous person living or dead,
would you sit on a park bench with and chat?
Maybe Jesus, or Buddha or …?
They can keep fame. I'd always pick you, Jimmy.
I'd tell you about our children and share their pictures.
You'd be so proud of how they turned out.
We have grandchildren.
They call you Grandpa Jim.
I know you like that.
It's the simple things I miss, our Saturday trips to the library,
Sitting in bed reading our books. You loved online quizzes,
And in one group the men played the women and whichever
team lost someone had to sing. Often I'd hear MEEMEE
coming from the study. Then I'd hear you sing.
Another favourite memory comes from our first Christmas
together.
Carols on the TV, Adeste Fidelis is coming next. Game on.
I belted out O Come all Ye faithful, and you set your inner
catholic schoolboy free and belted out Adeste Fidelis in Latin. It
may not have been melodic… but we laughed.
I wish I could sing it in Latin.
Memories are better than symbols and signs,
they bring joy tinged with sadness.

But Jimmy, if you want to reach out,
no feathers, no pennies.
Rather touch my hand or steal a kiss.

Linda Blackshaw

All Our Yesterdays

Years separated us, time not distance
our daughter bridging our parallel lives.
At the end, remnants of the past
drew us together again.

ICU, I'm listed next of kin

The empty years between us
fall away
as if we had spent
all our yesterdays together.

I'm here, hold my hand

Too old now for grievances
anger, hurt, a diminished memoir
heartbreak healed, scarred over
embers long burned to ashes.

We remember the comfort of love

Swift time canters on
inexorably, for both of us
time for redemption
old grudges forgiven.

Last kiss, a new ending

Maria Bonar

Bush Romance Villanelle

Magic days, aglow with passion's flame
when love was born and flared Venetian red
those carefree days will never come again

Joe wooed young Lily, swiftly staked his claim
coaxed and charmed away her maidenhead
magic days aglow with passion's flame

Well bred, good stock he judged, no featherbrain
Lil found herself wide-girthed and newlywed
those carefree days will never come again

He carried off his bride with new surname
now mistress of a distant old homestead
magic days, aglow with passion's flame

While mustering cattle on the western plain
thrown from his horse he landed on his head
those carefree days will never come again

On Father's Day they buried Joe McBain
Lil remembers that December they were wed
magic days aglow with passion's flame
those carefree days will never come again

Maria Bonar

Flame Tree

The flame tree stood on
the corner of the avenue.
Every year a delight
a riot of crimson blooms
to cheer the heart,
brighten the eye

like a vibrant new gown
on a young belle
at the high school ball.

Then it was gone.
 Chopped
    down
        stump   ground away.
A square transplant of lawn
erasing its very existence.

Maria Bonar

Found

Larksong sweetens the dawn
weary nurse, crumpled apron
veil askew, torch in hand

Another feverish digger arrives
arm sling looped around his neck
face camouflaged with mud and blood

"Is that you, Mary?" he asks

She throws her arms
around her brother, Tom
no longer missing in action.

Maria Bonar

Making Hay Sestina

This will be our time
from hearth into sunlight
a season to be wild
as the climbing red rose
secret yearnings will end
with the taste of honey

Yes, wine and honey
drowsy in summertime
at long afternoon's end
when golden sunlight
fades to dusky rose.
Makes blood run wild

as flames run wild.
Fire molten as honey
bees brew from the rose
in the warm noontime.
Sip nectar in sunlight
until evensong's end

Summer reaping will end.
Will this love in the wild
fade with the sunlight?
No more stolen honey
kisses, come autumn time
and the last withered rose

Only thorns on the rose
bush at autumn's end.
Surely there will be a time
again, when passions run wild
with the sly taste of honey
on our tongues in the sunlight?

Winter dark with little sunlight
only a memory of the rose.
Snowdrifts, dreams of honey
all that remain in the end,
desire to unwrap your wild
warm body this yule time.

Sunlight will return in the end
the rose will bloom in the wild
hay harvest, our honey time.

Maria Bonar

Moonlight Ghazal

Tiny jewels shine in the moonlight
like ruby red wine in the moonlight

She pirouettes in a shot silk gown
her dance steps divine in the moonlight

Campfire under the Southern Cross sky
five bright stars align in the moonlight

Sculpture shadows across Lake Ballard
salt lake crystalline in the moonlight

Driving her Holden down Greenmount Hill
the road serpentine in the moonlight

White cross, scattered flowers, teddy bears
by a roadside shrine in the moonlight

Bush band wedding in an outback town
kiss from Caroline in the moonlight

Maria Bonar

One Hundred and Two

for Ruth Reid

I bring her mangoes

her sight almost gone
her hearing too
mind diamond-sharp
body frail, tremorous
hirples along the corridor
with her Zimmer frame

I bring her mangoes

for their scent and taste
strawberries and blueberries
she saves them for her
breakfast cereal with
tea in sturdy cup
no more delicate china

I bring her mangoes

and new poems for her birthday
she dons her headphones
words amplified, I read to her
silver princess weeps
outside her window
she cannot see its beauty

Maria Bonar

Quick Exit

after Nude Descending a Staircase (No.2)
by Marcel Duchamp, 1912.

Naked, wearing only bruises
she flees down the staircase
dripping a spotted blood trail
on the wooden slats.

Yesterday's iris-bloom injuries
purple and yellow, overlaid
by tonight's cyanotic blue.
A necklace of thumbprints.

Her husband/tormenter/Janus
keeper of the key and doorways
snores sour alcoholic breaths
in the debris of their bedroom.

In this house, his true visage
revealed. Cruel, condescending
brutal, unlike the urbane cultured
face he presents to the world.

This time, the need for survival
outweighs her terror. In the hallway
snatches a raincoat, purse, his keys.
Takes money from his wallet.

Feet pushed into boots
stumbles her way to freedom
through the open doorway
and into the night.

Maria Bonar

Waiting

for Ruth Reid

I am weary, Lord.
Let me shed my earthly
bones and frail flesh
let them melt away.

I have the keys to the city.
Let me herd my sheep
across the bridge and
unlock the pearly gates.

Let my soul ascend
to the heavens and
the voice of Dame Joan
sing me home, sweet home.

Sight, sound, colour
and melody restored
I will traverse the cosmos
flit among the stars

gaze in wonder
at the Jewel Box,
the Necklace Nebula
and the Galactic Rose.

Beyond the ancient
fiery light of Venus
Planet Reid awaits
and a Gordon for me.

Maria Bonar

Notes:
1. Ruth Reid was a Freeman of the City of London, which granted her the right to herd sheep over London Bridge.
2. Former WA Governor, Gordon Reid and his wife Ruth had a planet named after them in 1993, to recognise their significant contribution to the community.

Western Front

Churned earth and winter grass
the plough reveals a tattered wallet
old money, a faded photograph

a Digger at peace for one hundred years
disturbed, skeletal gaze unearthed
a battered helmet, ruined khaki

long lost to family, now reclaimed
by a younger generation
cherished, named and framed.

Maria Bonar

Meh!

He stares at the television, day after day. Switched on or off, it makes no difference.

He hardly moves from his bed. Doesn't want to, nor sees a need to.

People turn up, look worried, ask stupid questions, give mindless information and leave. More people turn up, ask the same stupid questions. The answers seem of great importance to them, not him.

A home help appears, steals his sheets and washes them without permission.

He can no longer smell his late wife. He stops eating. A fruit bowl attracts flies with over-ripe bananas and soft, festering plums.

Erica Bowman

Stuck

James is utterly miserable. Stuck on frustrated. Four
thwarted attempts to get out of bed. What a life.
Finally, he's up – Scowling, growling, cursing at the kettle.
Bladder bursting, bones creaking, gas passing, glasses lost;
discovered in fridge. No milk. Black coffee the cure for excess
bourbon binging. Shoes not happening. James screams in rage.
He makes it outside. Trudges along. Drags his high-vis vest over
his miserable head.
The children come. Shrieks of laughter ensue. James holds back
the traffic like Moses parting the waves.
He grins widely at the children, who give him purpose and melt
his heart.

Erica Bowman

Across Two Worlds

Wide open skies and ochre land
Your rawness draws me in close
To see an ancient past firsthand

In rocks that look like waves I stand
Observe the curves of a past now lost
Wide open skies and ochre land

Below the earth are treasures grand
Symbolic art my eyes transpose
To see an ancient past firsthand

Around I seek to understand
A common ground, a spiritual host
Wide open skies and ochre land

Across two worlds I am spanned
I try to steer with different strokes
Wide open skies and ochre land
To see an ancient past firsthand

Aileen Boyer

Djeran

It's an in-between season
A mix of hot and cold
A summer kiss
An autumn mist
A colour twist and fold.
Winds of change
Signal growth
Time to mend, repair
As red rust shacks prepare
their seeded troth
And red flowering gum
And summer flame
Spread their glory
Into the story
And create
the Djeran frame.

Aileen Boyer

Fall Gal

"Not egg and chips for dinner again!"

She baulked at his reaction, watching the squishy yellow yoke hit the floor as he swept his plate out of her hand.

He hadn't always been an angry man. He had swept her off her feet with his gallantry and loving admiration, his gentle touch.

The derision had been a slow realisation all was not well. At first, she joked with him over her blunders, accepting her inadequacies. As they mounted, along with his insults and rejections mixed with protests of love, she knew all was not well. He insisted she was being unreasonable, that it was all in her head.

This time, the broken yolk of the egg broke inside her head.

She stooped to pick up the remains, but instead of binning the mess, she smeared it all over his disbelieving face before heading for the door.

She was no Humpty Dumpty. She could put herself together again.

Aileen Boyer

Out with the Old and In with the New

She squeezed past the pile of newspapers in the hallway, sliding her way into the kitchen.

This would be the year, she vowed. It had to stop. Soon, there would be no room left for her to get through. In her mind, she had already decided how it would be done. Oldest first. She picked up the first bundle, ready to apply her New Year's resolution. Out with the old and in with the new.

She heard the newspaper boy's familiar ring of the doorbell. Two long, two short. She had trained him well. It was the highlight of her day. She picked up the old bundle and headed to the front door to pick up her latest cache. She was about to drop the old papers from April 1984 into the recycle bin when something caught her eye. It was the year Advance Australia Fair became the national anthem. They had all celebrated and partied, believing in their future. She hummed the tune to herself, hugging the bundle close, remembering. She had lost them all in that fateful car crash.

She hadn't ventured far since then. Safer to be home. Kitchen and coffee. It was all too much. She took the bundle back inside before returning for her new comfort. The world was changing. She liked to read about it, but she wasn't ready to be in it, however much she would like to have space to move.

"Maybe next year," she sighed, before attempting her slide back into the kitchen.

Aileen Boyer

A Future With AI

The old dream was that one day, all the heavy, physical, mundane work would be done by robots, releasing humans to do the fun things. To travel, read, play sport or do creative stuff like art, music and literature.

We hailed it as progress when technology took the jobs of the bank tellers and checkout attendants, typographers and printers, telephone and television transmitter technicians. But now, even the creative activities are being taken over by AI. Soon, only the often messy jobs, like nursing or plumbing, will be available for humans.

We never really noticed AI creeping up on the arts. With typical human hubris, we believed it could never replace a real writer or artist, laughing scornfully at the multiple fingers and glassy eyes of its early attempts at representing people.

But its style rapidly improved and we enjoyed the harmless little movies of kittens, puppies and babies, sharing them on social media, and laughed to see politicians we love to hate in hilarious or embarrassing scenes. But how far can that go? It is getting hard to tell what is real. Could such manipulation sway public opinion?

Not only is AI getting smarter than us, it is frighteningly objective. It won't be distracted by love and other human concerns. It won't have to lose sleep over a child's illness, a spat with a partner or other family member. It won't get tired, and it won't get the blues.

No, AI will just carry on, picking human brains to learn more and more. Already, it can find, in minutes, data that would take a human researcher months, and it is learning to deconstruct a painting or a written text and replicate the style. It wasn't happy with designing book covers, now it's writing the books as well.

We looked the other way when it came for the animators, the graphic designers, the musicians and composers. Now, it's coming for us.

Lynne Cairns

Moon Madness

It was hard to get to sleep in the strange bed, with the moonlight so bright. Even as a child, I would wake screaming from half-remembered terrors on nights of the full moon. So, at home, I had heavy curtains to block the brightness.

I did finally get to sleep, but strange images flashed across my mind as the moon's light penetrated further into the room. It seemed to be calling to me, 'Come out, come out to me.' So I arose and walked out onto the lawn, feeling the cool dampness of dew on my bare feet. Out there, I could no longer resist.

My heart pumped blood through my veins, all my body hairs stood on end, and I raised my voice in praise of the night. Then I was running through the forest, filled with some wild joy and ancient instinct that overrode conscience and conscious thought.

When I awoke, it was still dark. Only fragments of the dream lingered, but there was a foul taste in my mouth, and my lips were encrusted with some ill-smelling substance. When I went to the bathroom and turned on the light, the full horror was revealed. Dried blood clung to my face and hands. Shuddering, I tried to scrub it off, but even when my skin was rubbed nearly raw, the damning evidence could not be erased from my fingernails.

I made some excuse to cut short my holiday and flew home. Now I watch the news continuously, waiting to hear that some horrible crime has been discovered in that forest.

Lynne Cairns

People Like Us

We should have noticed, been warned somehow, that it could happen to us. It was happening to people in other places, but the killing and the dying never seemed quite real. We'd seen it all before. The terrified families running from the bombs and the shelling, the broken bodies crumpled on the bloody, shattered pavement. We watched as missiles crashed into high-rise buildings, with never a thought that in every one of those rooms there could be a man, a woman, a child, a family, waiting to be blown apart.

It was as unreal to us as the violence we enjoyed in movies and sport. A kind of war games, reality TV show. And we loved our reality TV. We loved to see people fighting – over a man, a woman, a house, a chef's acclaim.

Politics was just another reality show – the ultimate non-contact sport. We loved the abuse and trickery, applauding the skill with which our team backpedalled, or deftly handballed blame. But we roared with self-righteous anger when someone stumbled. When the media, digging into private lives and pasts, found hidden secrets that could not only drive a politician from office, but might change the course of our history.

And it did.

Most of us welcomed the new government. Everything was going to be fixed. Crime and drug abuse would be abolished by the imposition of harsher penalties. Security was tightened. Terrorism was abroad, and we must be protected, so our police got more powerful weapons. The homeless disappeared, and a few annoying minority leaders, but we were secure in our gated communities.

Some of the new rules were annoying, of course. You were expected to carry ID and could be asked for it. CCTVs appeared on every building in the city, and armed guards inspected your ticket on the train.

Gunfire at night showed us how well we were being protected by the soldiers who patrolled the streets. As long as we stayed at home and obeyed the curfew, we knew we'd be safe.

Of course we conformed. It was for our own good after all, so we were annoyed when we heard people complaining. The whingers soon disappeared, though, so we could relax.

Until things started happening to people like us – seemingly at random.

Homes were invaded. Screaming people were dragged from their beds and taken away, or shot in front of their families, by masked, heavily armed men. No one could tell if they were soldiers or armed rebels. They all looked the same.

It was civil war, we were told. Nothing civil about it! Families split apart, some fighting on both sides.

Then the bombing began. Not just the occasional terrorist attack. We'd got used to them, with their homemade bombs, but these were the real thing. Professionally made. Fine engineering! Designed to pierce armour and anything else that stood in their way.

We never saw the ships or planes that sent them raining down on us. Homes were destroyed, and food disappeared from the shops. Sanctions, we were told.

***

Now we're here on this boat. Too many of us! The engines just sputtered and died. We drift towards the horizon, where dark storm clouds gather. My baby is crying. All the babies are crying.

'What's going to happen to us, Mummy?' my daughter whispers, but I have no answer to give her. All I can do is hold her close and pray.

Lynne Cairns

Super Comeback

Today was the first day of the rest of her life. After ten years of retirement, she'd discovered that the ailment she was suffering from was simply boredom.

After all, she hadn't really wanted to retire. It had been forced on her when she no longer fitted the image and the skin-tight costume the World Defenders were expected to wear, when her boobs began to droop and her tummy expanded, and her beautiful face gained a network of lines.

In the first weeks after she hung up her cape, she had revelled in freedom from responsibility for the world's troubles. She'd remodelled her house, replanted the garden, researched all her ancestors back to the year dot, and learned to paint and play the harpsichord, but her restless spirit hankered to use her powers as she always had.

When she was reduced to spending her days mindlessly scrolling through social media following the exciting lives of her successors in the industry, she decided to come out of retirement. But first, it had been necessary to design a new image.

After searching old legends and the gospels of ancient religions for images of men and women who had harnessed the might of the universe to strike their foes, she had devised an outfit that was, she hoped, suitably awe-inspiring.

So today was the big day. The day she would again use her superpowers for the benefit of humankind. But no longer would she be at the beck and call of those who had taken over World Defenders Inc. This time, she would be in complete control.

She would make her own decisions about what was needed to clean up the mess the world had got itself into while she had been looking the other way. She must have absolute freedom to decide who to save and who to eliminate.

Lynne Cairns

March Planting

For exactly one hundred and ninety years, the tree had stood in that spot, while the surrounding bush gave way to farms, and farms gave way to concrete and bitumen. Now the concrete and bitumen would win, despite the efforts of Mollie and her supporters.

Mollie wiped a tear from her eye, remembering her grandad's words, 'We always had a birthday party for the tree,' he'd laughed. 'Grandma insisted her mother, Letty, had planted her last acorn on the 17th of March, St. Patrick's Day, hoping he might bless the planting.'

The other five acorns she had carried across the wild seas hadn't taken in the alien soil, but people who'd weathered a few years of this land's topsy-turvy seasons, said to wait for the first rains. So she'd waited. March was supposed to be when the seasons changed, but two weeks went by, and the thirsty soil still ached for relief from the searing summer heat. Then the skies opened, and for three days it rained.

Then, on the seventeenth, when the sun smiled on the newly washed earth, Letty dug a wee hole in the newly soaked soil and popped in the last acorn, or so the story went.

Mollie looked at the six acorns in her hand. She hoped she'd chosen well, for they were to be the oak tree's legacy, growing old in peace, she hoped, around her new home in the country.

Lynne Cairns

New Beginnings (Part 2)

On August 31 1976, my family migrated from UK to Western Australia. The ten-pound passage was phasing out, so we paid for our own fares on a Jumbo Jet. Our family consisted of me, aged thirty-eight, my husband, aged forty-one, our son, aged seventeen, our daughter, aged fifteen, and our youngest son, aged seven. We emerged from the plane wearing hiking boots. This was because we had just spent a walking holiday in Perth, Scotland, and I insisted that everyone wear the expensive, heavy boots to avoid the excess baggage charges.

Because of the currency restrictions in UK our finances were restricted, so we decided to accept the offer of accommodation in Noalimba, a government hostel in an area called Bateman, south of the Swan River. Our first impressions on the drive to the hostel were of the detached 'bungalows' which contrasted with English houses, where, unless you were wealthy, they were either terraced or semi-detached. We left London in the midst of a heat wave; the countryside was parched and brown, and there were water restrictions. An old age pensioner was fined for watering her vegetables with a handheld hose in London. It was the rainy season in Perth, but later I thought it incredible that so much valuable water was lavished on the gardens.

At the hostel, we were welcomed, and the advice they gave was invaluable. It also gave us a breathing space to look around for a place to settle, and to research business prospects. We were advised to make a will, which I thought was somewhat morbid. At that time, we were entitled to draw the dole.

The manager said, "Don't feel guilty, you'll soon be paying your taxes." His predictions were only too accurate.

We were allotted three adjacent rooms with shared ablution facilities, and dined buffet-style in a communal cafeteria. The food was wholesome and well-cooked, though some people whinged without cause. A school bus took the children to and from school. The communal life cushioned the culture shock of the new environment, and it was one of the perks to hear gossip in the laundry rooms. At this time, we were free of a mortgage, so my husband told the manager, "If you had a swimming pool here, I'd stay forever."

A disadvantage of the hostel was noisy neighbours, although most inmates were considerate. One day, a Scottish migrant named Robbie Burns arrived. His first words were "Where can I get a drink?" He had brought his guitar, and although he was talented, it was annoying that he sang and played until the early hours, disturbing those who had to get up at the crack of dawn. One night, he must have had an argument with his wife because he banged on her door, shouting, "Maggie! Maggie! Let me in!". In the morning, we found him propped up against the door, sound asleep. The chutzpah was that we were summoned to the manager's office. "Robbie Burns has complained that you have your TV on too loud." The manager announced with a wry smile. My husband was fuming, and although Robbie was a strapping six-foot labourer, he confronted him.

"It was just that I wanted to be moved somewhere quiet so I can play my guitar without anyone disturbing me," Robbie told him.

About this time, the eight weeks allocated for our stay were up. We had found a house and a place to start a business. Also, we made good friends, and our children were adapting to life in Australia. It was fortuitous that we decided to enjoy our last week of freedom because, during our first year, we had to contend with problems. Our furniture was destroyed because of water leaking into the container, and my husband suffered from a serious bout of pneumonia.

Fortunately, we cannot foretell the future so we visited the tourist spots, appreciated the beautiful scenery, and marvelled at the exotic plants and animals. One morning we explored Swanbourne beach, which was almost deserted because Australians don't usually swim until the sweltering summer months. We'd been acclimatised to the English temperature and the sea looked inviting.

"You can swim in the altogether here, it's a nudist beach," my husband said.

"When in Rome do as the Roman's do," I said as I stripped off, followed by my husband. Together we plunged into the surf. Although cold, we felt euphoric as we shook off the inhibitions of our past and immersed ourselves in the new life.

Pat Curtis

Day One

A shrill *BEEP BEEP* startled Bec into consciousness. Her hand jerked from beneath the duvet to slam off the alarm clock.

Why the hell did I set that?

Her head foggy, she rolled over and closed her eyes. Then she remembered. *Oh shit. Today's the appointment.*

With a groan, she kicked off her covers and creaked out of bed. She wasn't sure what time she'd passed out, but the fuzz of intoxication hadn't quite left her body. The sound of the toilet flushing told her that her housemate, Taylor, hadn't gone to work yet. Bec considered waiting, but the appointment was at nine, and she had to get there on the bus … so she shuffled into the kitchen.

Taylor sat at the table, scrolling her phone as she munched toast. "Morning, Bec. I was about to come and wake you."

Bec switched on the kettle. "Do you want a coffee?"

"I've already had one. There's extra toast if you want some."

Bec grunted and reached for the coffee jar. When she went to grab a teaspoon from the drawer, she noticed a crushed cardboard box in the recycling bin.

Her heart rate quickened. "Where's the wine that was in that?"

"Down the drain. You told me to throw the rest of your booze away after last night, remember? Today is meant to be your first day sober."

Bec's face flushed. She gripped the sink to steady her hands. "Oh, yeah."

Brushing crumbs from her chin, Taylor rose and walked over to pat Bec's back. "You *need* to do this, Bec. Things will never get better if you don't. Now, eat something."

Bec finished her breakfast and, on Taylor's insistence, took a quick shower. Taylor also insisted upon dropping Bec off at the bus station, despite there being a stop not far from their unit. In the passenger's seat of Taylor's Corolla, Bec slouched and picked at her cuticles. Her mouth felt like stale beef jerky, and tasted like it, too.

"I don't feel well," Bec said as Taylor pulled into a parking spot.

"What else is new? Your withdrawals shouldn't be too bad this time, since I've been keeping my eye on you. There's Panadol in your bag. Drink lots of water."

For Bec's latest attempt at sobriety, Taylor had appointed herself Bec's personal detox nurse. She'd taken Friday off from her job before a long weekend to supervise Bec and ensure she didn't start drinking too early in the day. Over the past four days, she'd managed to wean Bec from three litres of wine a day down to less than one, although Bec had sneaked in a couple of extra glasses here and there. Having endured Bec's outlandish behaviour during her numerous binges over the two years they'd been living together, Taylor was determined to help her friend do things differently this time. She hoped this would result in Bec changing for the better; otherwise, she'd be looking for a new housemate.

She nudged Bec's shoulder. "You'll be fine. Off you go before you miss your bus."

Bec cracked open her door. "I'll see you this afternoon."

She joined the queue for the city express and snaffled a seat along the back row. Her stomach squirmed when the bus took off. She popped two tablets from the sachet Taylor had given her, gulped half a bottle of water, then squashed in her earbuds.

According to Google Maps, Bec's intended destination was 400 metres from the stop where she alighted. It took her less than the predicted time to walk to the two-storey building. The words *Tranquil House Outpatient Centre* gleamed from the glass door in silver block letters, above the symbol of a tree with its branches spread wide like a jumble of open arms.

The receptionist buzzed her in, took her details, and within minutes, Bec was in a therapy room. A trio of armchairs gathered around a low, rectangular table filled most of the space. The obligatory box of tissues adorned the middle of the table, along with a frosty metal jug and two full glasses.

Counsellor Mandy flipped through pages in her notebook as she perched on the edge of her seat. "I've read through your case notes, but I'd like to hear why *you* think you're here, and what you hope to get out of this. And please be honest. There's no judgment here."

Bec adjusted the cushion behind her back. "I got caught drink driving and the court referred me."

Mandy nodded. "Was this the first time you've driven whilst under the influence of alcohol or other substances?"

Bec's eyes wandered sideways. "No…"

"Just the first time you've been arrested."

"Yeah." Bec smirked. "I crashed my car *directly in front* of the police station."

"That was unlucky." Mandy glanced at her notes. "Has your drinking ever caused any problems with your work, school or relationships?"

Bec bit her lip. "I got fired for drinking at my last job, but it wasn't completely my fault. And my housemate has threatened to kick me out, too."

Mandy's pen scratched on the paper. "How much do you drink and use other drugs?"

Bec rattled off the answers she'd given in numerous sessions with previous therapists. "At least two litres of wine a day, sometimes more. Sometimes other drinks like vodka or bourbon. I occasionally take pills and smoke pot."

"Do you think drinking is affecting your ability to get another job?"

Bec sighed. "Probably. But once I *do* get one, I'll have something to do during the day, and drink less."

Mandy hummed. "But you told me you used to drink while you were *at* work. Did you work in a place that served alcohol?"

"No, but it was stressful, and I got into a complicated situation. I'd make sure it didn't happen again."

"Have you ever tried to reduce or stop drinking?"

Bec curled a strand of golden hair around her finger. "There have been times I got really sick and didn't drink for a few days afterwards. I did an inpatient detox for a week a couple of years ago and have seen a few psychologists. I've been able to control it for short periods, and only drink after work and on weekends, but something *always* happens, and I end up drinking all day, every day again."

Mandy flipped her long, dark ponytail over her shoulder. "Do you think that perhaps you need to stop drinking and using other drugs completely?"

Bec slumped. "Maybe, but I don't think I can. Life gets depressing and it's impossible to have fun. That's why I end up drinking again."

"*I* haven't used for almost nine years, and my life is far from depressing. There are good and bad times, of course, but overall things are much better now than when I was using."

Bec lifted her head. "*You* used to use drugs?"

Mandy nodded. "I stopped when I was twenty-five, the same age you are. I also went through *Tranquil House*."

Cogs began to turn in Bec's brain. She gazed at Mandy, wondering whether she was telling the truth.

Mandy crossed one of her slender legs over the other. "You may have read that the *Tranquil House* program is based on complete abstinence from all drugs and alcohol. This is why we encourage participants to attend one of our rehab facilities, if it's feasible for them. You'll be somewhere safe, where you can't use, and be supported by a like-minded community."

Bec circled her feet on the carpet. "I *did* read about it, but I don't think I'd last eight months at a rehab. Not with no smoking or phones or internet. I need to focus on getting a job so I can pay for my car to get fixed and get on with my life."

Mandy pursed her lips. "Okay. Do consider it, though."

For the remainder of the hour, Bec recounted her drinking history to yet another health professional. She didn't have to think much about the story anymore, except to add the latest drama. Her stomach writhed, and before the session finished, she had to excuse herself to throw up.

Locked in the bathroom, Bec examined her reflection. Her face resembled a hospital bedsheet that had been washed too many times. Blotches of sweat soaked through the armpits of her pink shirt. With trembling hands, she smoothed her tangled hair.

Mandy offered a glass of water when Bec returned. "Feeling better?"

Bec coughed on the acid in her throat as she took a sip. "A bit."

"What have you got planned for the rest of the day?"

"Not much."

"That's dangerous. Have you ever been to a Narcotics Anonymous meeting?"

Bec's eyes narrowed. "Is it like Alcoholics Anonymous? My housemate dragged me there once. It was okay, but everyone was old, and it seemed like some kind of religious cult."

Mandy laughed. "Fair comment. There's a younger crowd in NA, and it *can* seem cult-like at first, but I think you should give it a chance. If you're up to it, there's a meeting on in a couple of hours, just down the road from here. I can go with you."

"What am I going to do until then?"

"You can stay here and browse our library. It's not too exciting but very educational. Otherwise, there's the shopping centre down the road, and a couple of op shops. Try to avoid the bottle store, obviously."

Bec's gut gurgled as she rested her hand on it. "I'll see how I feel. Can I hang out in the waiting room for a bit?"

"Sure."

With a cup of coffee, cold water, and more Panadol, Bec's symptoms settled. As much as she didn't want to admit it, Taylor's gradual reduction method seemed to have made this round of withdrawals more manageable. Although a large part of her wanted to rush off to the nearest pub (which she'd observed was a few hundred metres down the street), she didn't have the energy. The staff let her be, pausing intermittently to check whether she needed anything. Other clients, some of whom looked as peaky as Bec, nipped in and out of appointments.

Eventually, Bec mustered the strength to go outside for a cigarette. She walked around the block while she smoked, appreciating the fresh mist of drizzle in the air. It wasn't long before Mandy reappeared, and the two women set off.

They crossed a leafy park and headed to a hall behind an old church. Half a dozen people gathered the required distance from the doors, chatting while they smoked and vaped. Bec followed Mandy inside to join the eclectic array of attendees: some wearing sports-brand hoodies and trackpants; others in smart business attire; girls who looked barely out of high school; a bunch of folks in their thirties, and a man who reminded Bec of her grandfather. Positioned in a huge circle that spanned the entire room were plastic chairs, like the ones Bec had used in high school. In the middle of the circle was a table, where a redheaded man with a ghoulish skull tattoo on his left forearm sat.

He jingled a bell, and the room silenced.

"My name is Shane and I'm an addict. Welcome to the lunchtime meeting of Narcotics Anonymous."

"Hi, Shane," said everyone in the room.

Shane began with a *Welcome to Country* and told people where the facilities were, then read a few passages from a blue-covered book. All the attendees, including Mandy, chanted along with some of his words. Bec wrapped her arms around herself and studied the ground. Then, one by one, everyone introduced themselves and said how long they'd been clean. The older gentleman claimed to be 31 years clean. The majority had a few weeks or months clean; some, like Mandy, had a few years. Then it was Bec's turn.

Mandy whispered, "Just say your name and that you're clean today."

Bec's cheeks burned."I'm Bec. I'm clean today."

"Hi, Bec," boomed her fellow participants.

"Is it your first meeting?" asked Shane.

"Yes…"

Everyone burst into applause. Mandy prodded Bec. "Go up and get a tag."

"What?"

"It's okay, I'll come to you." Shane pushed his chair back and strode across the room with a white keyring dangling from his finger. He shook Bec's hand as he presented it to her."Welcome."

Bec tucked it into her pocket without making eye contact with him. "Thanks."

After stewing in embarrassment for several minutes, Bec zoned out. She caught snippets of shares, however, her thoughts constantly strayed. Although people described the unpleasant consequences of their using, it initiated Bec's cravings. It had been over twelve hours since her last drink. Her body longed for something to relieve its ache. She jiggled on the uncomfortable chair while the skin on her arms felt as though there were bugs crawling underneath it.

Should I head to the nearest bottle shop after this? Or go to the one closer to home, so I don't have to lug a cask on the bus? But I promised Taylor I wouldn't drink anymore...

Shane's voice pierced her thoughts. "Bec, would you like to share?"

Bec shuddered. "No!"

"No problem. Welcome again."

A murmur of 'Welcome' and 'Keep coming back' droned through the room.

Bec let her hair fall around her face as she looked at her lap. *Are these people for real? Could I ever be like them?*

The next speaker, a woman maybe ten years older than Bec, said something that captured Bec's attention: "If you do what you've always done, you'll get what you've always got. I had to risk doing something different, despite how frightening it was. *That's* when the real change happened."

After the meeting ended, that same woman approached Mandy and Bec with a bright smile on her face.

Mandy hugged her. "Good to see you, Justine."

"You too. And welcome, Bec. This could be the first day of your new life."

Mandy chuckled. "Don't overwhelm her. Just getting to a meeting is a big step."

"True. For an addict, one day clean is a miracle. You can leave here and never use again."

Bec stepped backwards. *What's this chick on? Oh, that's right – nothing.* "Okay."

Mandy checked her watch. "I need to get back. Will you be all right to get home from here, Bec?"

Justine whipped out her phone. "Let me give you my number."

Bec folded her arms. "You don't have to do that."

"It's good to get numbers. I'm off, but you hang around, Bec. Bye, guys." Mandy scooted.

Bec fumbled for her phone and exchanged numbers with Justine. *What's this all about? What does she want from me?*

Shane finished locking up the hall. "A few of us are going for lunch across the road. Everyone's welcome to join us."

Justine headed after him. "Sounds great. Come with us, Bec."

"I haven't got much money."

"My shout. What else are you going to do? Use?" Bec's eyes widened. Justine grinned. "It takes one to know one."

Bec shrugged a shoulder. "I was thinking about it."

Justine bundled Bec along. "Come on. It's early. You can use after lunch, if you still want to."

Bec lit a cigarette as the group traipsed along the footpath. "How long have you been clean?" she asked Justine.

"Four and a half years."

"And you haven't used *anything* in that time?"

"Nope. No drugs, no booze."

"Did you go to rehab?"

"That wasn't for me. I just did meetings. It took me a few tries to get my first six months up, but I kept coming back."

Bec flicked ash. "In the meeting, people were talking about sponsors, and working the steps..."

Justine held up her hand. "Don't worry about that yet. Just keep coming to meetings, and don't pick up. Things will make more sense in time."

***

That afternoon, Taylor returned home to find Bec sprawled on the sofa watching a comedy. Her nose twitched as she went for the fridge. The *thuck* of its door being yanked open drifted to the lounge.

Taylor returned and glanced around the room. "No wine?"

"No wine."

Taylor sank onto the arm of the couch. "Your appointment went well, then?"

Bec paused the film and recounted the details of her day. Taylor's face glowed when Bec showed off her white keyring.

"Amazing. You prefer NA to AA, then?"

"Not sure. It still seems like a cult. Everyone's super friendly as though they've been brainwashed."

Taylor snickered. "Maybe your brain *needs* washing."

"Maybe. Anyway, I agreed to go to another meeting tonight. Someone's picking me up at six. I made chilli con carne for dinner."

Taylor touched Bec's forehead. "So you're feeling okay? No bad withdrawals?"

Bec wiped her nose. "I've been better, but I'll live."

The evening meeting was much like the lunchtime one, except there were fewer people. In the candlelit room, Bec felt comfortable to share for a few moments. By the time she arrived home, her phone was full of new contacts. Bec put her head on the pillow, stunned that she had made it a whole day without drinking.

Ros Day

Mavis – My Gift to Me

Mavis was giving herself a Christmas gift. It was a gift that would be life-changing for her and the family, although they didn't know it yet.

The family arrived for Christmas lunch even though Mavis had tried to talk them out of it. As usual, her son Stephen had talked over her on the phone as Mavis was trying to tell him why.

"Don't be silly, Mum; we always come to you for Christmas lunch"

"Son, there is something I want to tell you..."

Stephen cut in, "I'm busy, Mum; we'll talk on Christmas Day," and promptly disconnected the phone.

Oh well, thought Mavis, *it'll be the last lunch.* There would be no more stressing about it after this year, no more cooking, food shopping and cleaning up afterwards, not that it was appreciated. Where had she and Rex gone wrong? How she missed her darling Rex. He'd passed away five years ago, and she still missed him. That seemed to be when Stephen, their only son, became entitled and opinionated. His wife, Kylie, wasn't much better – beautiful but aloof. Mavis always felt a little intimidated and dowdy beside her. As for the grandchildren, Jane, 15 and Troy, 13, they were downright rude at times, seeming to prefer their phones to real people.

Mavis had cooked a traditional Christmas lunch, complete with roast pork, ham, seafood, vegetables, salads, and the Christmas pudding. Lunch dragged on for Mavis. Stephen and Kylie talked nonstop about their lives and name-dropped like nobody's business. Every time Mavis made a comment, they smiled at her and kept talking. The children said nothing, annoyed that they weren't able to have their phones at the table.

At last, the meal was over. Stephen and Kylie headed for the lounge room. Mavis started to clear the table; no one offered to help. She sighed and tidied up the remnants of the lunch, taking her time because she knew what the conversation was going to be about. Finally, she made her way to the lounge. Lately, they had been trying to convince her to sell the house and move into a retirement home. Maybe she would get a chance to tell them what she had done now.

Mavis smiled at them both and said, "Now that we are all here, there is something I'd like to talk to you both about. I've..." That was as far as she got before Stephen interrupted.

"Well, Mum, we really must talk about you moving. This place is too big for you on your own."

Yes," chimed in Kylie, "you're not getting any younger."

Mavis bristled; she did all her own housework, gardening and was very active in the community. She didn't have a cleaner or gardener like Kylie.

"Well, I've some news..." she started again, only to be interrupted by Stephen again.

"Mum, this is more important. We can sell this house – it should sell for quite a bit – and move you into a nice, quiet retirement home. I can manage the sale, find a home and look after your finances for you."

Mavis tried to hide her smile and said, "Thank you for your concern. I know you mean well and have my best interests at heart, although I dispute the fact that I can't cope on my own and, as Kylie so kindly pointed out, I'm not getting any younger. So I agree with you, but I need to tell you..."

"That's great, Mum ..." He and Kylie smiled at each other. This had been easier than they thought. "We'll sort out things when we get back from our holiday in Bali. Did we tell you that we will be away for about two weeks?"

"Yes, dear, you did, and I hope you have a wonderful time, but I'd like to tell you..."

"Can we go yet?" Jane's whining voice interrupted.

"Well, yes, we should be going. We have drinks with the Thompsons across the road tonight," replied Kylie, and they piled out the door and into their swanky new BMW. Mavis sighed. *Peace at last.*

***

The next day, Elsie and Jack from next door popped over for a cuppa and a piece of Mavis's homemade Christmas cake.

"Well, how did they take the news?" asked Jack, blowing on his tea.

"As you know, I've been trying to tell them for over a month now, but haven't been able to get a word in, so they still don't know. In fact, they are planning to sell the house, find me a retirement home, not even a retirement village, and manage my money. I'm so angry that I mean so little to them." Tears escaped from her eyes. "How did it come to this? I miss Rex so much."

Elsie rose and hugged her friend, "It's OK, Jack and I are still here, and you'll only be a couple of streets away. We miss Rex as well. He'll be turning in his grave at the way they are treating you."

"Thanks, Elsie, I'm OK. I'll be moved into my new home by the time they get back from Bali."

Jack grinned, and then all three looked at each other and burst into laughter.

"Yes, it's all arranged, the house is sold to a lovely young couple with two small children, and Rex would like that. I've decided what I'm taking and what I'm donating to the Salvation Army. The movers are coming in three days; they will pack, move and unpack at the retirement village. As you say, it is only a couple of streets away and really lovely, … well, you have seen it. The lawyer is redoing my will; it turns out he was a little concerned so contacted me regarding Stephen wanting to know what his inheritance would be when I'm gone. As you both know Rex and I willed everything to each other. He has also put me onto a financial adviser who will look after any investments.

"After all, the money came from my parents' estate, which is how we were able to buy this house and set up Rex's business. Rex insisted that everything be kept in my name. Stephen did inherit some money from Rex's estate, but he doesn't know that the rest is mine. The lawyer has set it up so that Stephen and Kylie can't touch anything. I think they are in for a bit of a shock when I leave this earth."

"Mavis, old girl, what a lark! Rex would be proud of you, and you'll still be here living life to the fullest, and maybe even do that trip you have been promising yourself." Jack laughed again. "I can't wait to see their faces when they get back from Bali and come around for their usual Sunday roast lunch, and a stranger opens the door!

"What a unique Christmas present you have given yourself. A new home!

Lynne Doyle

Waiting

The early morning sun painted the station's chimneys gold. The air smelled crisp and clean. Justine had wakened before dawn when the wind was quiet, the countryside still except for the first bird calls. After yesterday's rain, sunshine bathed the highlands; a perfect day for his arrival.

Nestled in a valley, heather-covered hills, mountains, and streams surround the Crianlarich station. Mr Williamson, better known as Willy, stuck his head out of the ticket window. Justine knew she was early.

"The 10.49 train is not due for another twenty minutes. It will be on time – never comes early or late."Are you catching or waiting?"

"Waiting."

"Those poor beggars in London copped it again last night. Them Jerries just missed Saint Pauls Cathedral," Willy chatted on as Justine moved away.

Home, family, memories – all gone after one bombing raid; now Richard arrives by train.

***

The platform seemed like an empty stage waiting for the players to arrive. Justine smoothed a hand over her long skirt for the umpteenth time. Yesterday she had tried on several outfits – it would be important to make an impression. Finally, she'd decided on the tweed skirt and jacket. It would be a better choice than slacks. She tied back her auburn shoulder-length hair with a pretty scarf, thinking a hat would make her look like a schoolteacher.

Seven years had passed. Justine had been eighteen when she'd left London finding a new love and life in Scotland. There had been no communication between her and Richard – until the letter had arrived from the war office. Now in ten minutes he would be here.

She recalled his face: the blue eyes, thick blond curls … She glanced at the photo, years old now, and he would have changed.

***

Willy appeared on the platform as a lingering whistle trilled through the hills. Her stomach lurched at the first sight of the billowing smoke tail.

"Right on time." He smiled, touched his cap and returned to the ticket office.

In a few minutes, he would stand before her. She wondered what he would be thinking. Scotland would be so different from the London life he'd been used to. She had meant to write, keep in touch, but life and the war got in the way. Her knees trembled. She mustn't let her nerves get the better of her.

***

Smoke poured from the train as it pulled into the station, doors banging, steam filling the air.

"All aboard!" shouted Willy. He blew his whistle and waved the red flag. The powerful engine, a black mass, strained, spewed steam, and roared along the tracks, disappearing into the mountains.

He stood, a forlorn figure at the end of the platform, cap in hand, a small battered brown suitcase by his feet. His borrowed clothes were far too big and gave him a clown-like appearance. He was tall for his ten years. He held out his hand as she approached him.

"Hello, I am Richard." His voice cracked and his bottom lip quivered.

Justine ignored the outstretched hand and gathered him to her. The wait for her little brother was over – only three when she had left, and now he was here. He had cropped blond curls now, but his blue eyes, now brimming with tears, stared into hers. Her finger traced the scar down his cheek. He had survived that terrible night.

"Come on, let's go home. You have a five-year-old nephew who is dying to meet you."

Richard's smile stole her heart. He clasped her hand in his and together they walked past a smiling Willy.

June Earle

The Watcher in The Mall

Beneath the tree, in the canopy of shade, he sits. Man and the bench merges as one. He comes to the seat when the weather allows him to be part of its day.

He watches the comings and goings of life in the mall, struggling to adapt to the new world.

He listens to the sounds of everyday life. Clinking cups. The scream of coffee beans being devoured into the machine. A barista shouting orders. The city sweeper approaches its rotating brushes suck up debris. Papers and leaves whirl – escape proves futile.

A service vehicle honks, pedestrians scatter, but not the businessman. Briefcase in one hand, phone in the other, he was oblivious to his surroundings. Almost upon him, the truck emits another blast of its horn. The man makes a hasty retreat. The watcher laughs and salutes the driver.

He removes his cap and scratches his head through a crop of snow-white hair. His face was an age map, lines sinking into furrows of worn skin. Wiry brows hover over pale blue eyes. He pulls a pipe and makings from his pocket, taps the pipe on the bench to empty ash, ignores the mall's No Smoking signs. He fills the pipe and lights up; the sweet smell of the tobacco floats around him.

Two young ladies in short shorts are window shopping. Their attention focuses on ripped jeans in the latest fashion. He scrunches his face in disapproval of the tattoos that adorn their arms and legs.

Above well-worn, brown, polished shoes, his white socks gleam like a lighthouse beacon. His pinstriped navy suit is old and frayed on the cuffs and neckline. The clean white shirt, now grey with use, finishes the tidy ensemble. His appearance is that of a meticulous person, someone used to order and routine.

A busker sets up nearby. Dreadlocks crown a youthful face and dribble down his back in odd lengths, a new age person – would have been a hippie in his youth. Stripped baggy cotton trousers, red blouse, and yellow waistcoat flap over bare feet. He plays a violin. The old face shows surprise. A small crowd gathers, seduced by the music.

The melody smooths out surrounding sounds. The capped head slumps. Is he dreaming of a young man dancing to this tune with a beautiful girl in his arms?

The music stops. He wakes, relights his pipe, and continues watching.

June Earle

Station to Suburbia

Downsizing generally means moving from a large house to a smaller home or unit. For my husband and me, it has meant the transition from a million-acre cattle station to a suburban block.

It's been made a little easier, having bought our home in Leeming some years ago and renting to our daughter working in the city. Instead of paying for accommodation, we now had a permanent base on visits to Perth. This was invaluable when my husband had a health issue, which required some weeks spent in Perth.

My husband always planned to retire at 65 and hand the station management to our two sons, so 2023 saw us settle full-time into city life.

The move has been easier for me, as I'm a very social person who likes to be involved in things. I've joined a gym, become part of a coffee group and book club, as well as doing some volunteer work.

Still having the property is a lifeline for my husband, as he can, at times, return to the place his heart will always belong. He is also doing some volunteering. His other role is as the 'gopher' for the boys, finding parts, tools and other station requirements.

We have, since our move, had the opportunity to travel to areas of our state we hadn't previously visited. Getting away from a station was never an easy task.

Whilst we have both settled in well to life in Leeming, there are aspects of our former life we will always miss. The wide, open spaces and the amazing night skies can never be replicated down here. We keep one section of our bedroom blinds open at night so we can see the occasional star.

The city is never silent – how could it possibly be? At the station, there are days when not a sound disturbs the peace – no vehicles, animals, planes, birds, or generator (as we have solar power).

The freedom to walk out your door and not have to worry about locks and keys is something I took for granted over my forty years on the station. Don't tell my husband, but I have, since downsizing, been known to leave our back door unlocked or the garage door up on occasion.

We've pondered over sorting household rubbish here in the city. Does it go in the green bin, red bin, or yellow pin? Previously, we would put it in the chook bucket, feed it to the dog or cows, keep it 'just in case' or burnt it in a drum out back.

Shopping is now a low-key affair that can be done once a week or fortnightly, knowing we can nip back if we forget something. Just a tad different from a 420-kilometre round trip that we did from the station, filling the car to the brim and hoping we hadn't forgotten anything.

Retirement life is very different and combining it with such an enormous change of location has had its challenges but on the 10th July 2024, the arrival of our first grandchild, a beautiful little girl born to our daughter and son-in-law here in Perth, has brought us a whole new level of joy and can't imagine being thousands of kilometres away from her. So we look back with pride at our achievements whilst looking forward with anticipation.

Raelene Hall

Raelene has published two books of humorous short stories based on her station life, Legitimate Bush Woman, and Legitimate Bush Woman Goes to Town.

When Change is Forgotten

He forgot his change.

Correction – she forgot his change.

Cassie should chase after him. He'd given her a fifty-dollar note for his coffee. She'd blushed at his handsomeness and ducked her head down to fumble with notes in the drawer. People didn't use cash much anymore. Her fringe fell over her eyes, so she hadn't noticed him leaving while she was still counting.

"Cassie?"

She jumped, closing the till drawer with a bang. Her manager's voice was like ice water to the face.

"Can you take the next order?" Sally cocked her head to the long queue of uncaffeinated stares.

She couldn't race out of the store now on some crazed mystery dash after a stranger. Sally would drag her right back. "Yep." Cassie smiled at the first person in line, a puffer-vested lady who wanted tea with the bag left in. She pushed down the button of the kettle to boil the water and waited.

Would he come back? He would remember, surely? It was a lot of money. She had never seen him in here before, she would remember that jet black hair, the sharp edge of his jaw, those bright blue eyes. Why wasn't she friendlier? She cringed at how she had avoided eye contact.

"Cassie!"

Sally's reprimand this time jolted Cassie out of her daydreaming like the sharp yank of a full rubbish bag out of the bin. Sally was usually more patient, but it was a Saturday. Cassie shook her mind fog away and returned to the blinking order tablet and the line of unblinking customers.

***

Stephen didn't really drink coffee but he'd walked past Cuppa Café last weekend and seen the girl with the heavy bangs and bright red lips behind the counter. She was there again today. He'd walked in without a plan and asked for the first thing on the chalkboard – a flat white?

She hadn't looked up at him as she tapped in "tall" for size and "normal" for milk but he'd wanted to say – like me! – to see if she would giggle.

He didn't know the etiquette, so he'd stepped aside while his order was being made. There were no free stools. She beckoned him back for payment. He hated being so clumsy, and he quickly handed over a note from his wallet and fled, the failure of his wordless flirting heavy in his step.

He took a sip from the takeaway cup and grimaced. He forgot to ask for sugar.

***

"See you tomorrow."

Cassie gave a fluttery wave and heard Sally lock the door of the exhausted café behind her.

"Any chance of some sugar?"

Cassie stopped buttoning her coat. It was the man from earlier.

"You!"

Stephen flinched at her tone, catching her eye with his confusion. "Sorry, I meant actual sugar. That was a poor attempt at a joke, I ordered a coffee from you earlier today."

Cassie laughed. "No, it's okay, I remember. I've been

69

wondering how to track you down all day!"

Stephen raised an eyebrow. "I was trying to think of an excuse to come back."

One corner of Cassie's mouth curved upwards like the Nike swoosh. "You didn't need one. You forgot your change." She pulled out the money.

"Oh – thanks," Stephen said, folding the notes into his pocket. "That will cover me for a few more coffees. When are you working next?"

"Tomorrow." Cassie's heart rolled over at Stephen's grin. "And remember, the sugar comes free."

"I hope there's a time when I don't have to ask for it."

This time, Cassie didn't try to hide her blush.

Caroline Hayward

Changing Friendships

"Do you have to analyse everything?" Claire's husband asked.

She's thought about this question quite a bit over the years, which suggests that perhaps she does. In fact, it's our shared predisposition for the examined life that's the basis of our friendship. Claire's in her nineties, and I'm in my seventies, so, of late, we've been analysing changes in friendship as we age. We ask questions like:

- If the 'grumpy old man syndrome' is a real biological thing as testosterone declines, do we really want to spend time with miserable old blokes?

- What can we do about friends who become reclusive or aggressive as they get older?

- How do we meet new friends in retirement?

Health starts to dominate friendships in older years. I used to share a laugh in emailed jokes, but now two friends with macular degeneration can't read them. Horizons narrow – some friends no longer drive, and cataracts prevent others from driving at night. In younger years, my idea of hell was being locked in a room for eternity with all my friends. I'd worry that they wouldn't get on because some are passionately right- or left-wing in their political persuasions, and others range from spiritual Buddhists to hard-bitten 'rugger buggers'. But now we've mellowed. No more raging debates, just organ recitals as we garner information from each other about joint replacements, stents, and arthritis.

I now live a sedate social life. I've taken to inviting friends to watch a late afternoon movie on one of my streaming services followed by a quick meal so that we can be home and in bed before falling asleep in the armchair. I'm still laughing at a scene in the film we watched last week. A police profiler explained to detectives that the criminal was probably an autodidact. "So, he works in the car industry", the TV detective concluded. I thought this hilarious, but one friend didn't know what an autodidact is, and the other didn't hear the joke. She needs hearing aids but won't get them, and I forgot to put on the subtitles – and she didn't ask. I might just as well have been on my own.

I can tell when friends are losing their hearing because they ask me questions about what I've just said, but I've concluded, without certainty, that when friends start talking over me, they're not being rude. They just didn't hear what I was saying – or maybe they weren't listening – or both.

Luke emailed to chat about his hiking weekend in the Yorkshire Dales. He despaired of his friends.

"They were mainly couples, but only one couple exhibited any overt warmth or closeness to each other. The rest? You wouldn't have thought they were together! One friend was impatient with potential criticism boiling just below the surface. She was a simmering fight-picker for the whole of our hiking trip. Her husband copped a lot of it for absolutely no discernible reason. Her behaviour bordered on bullying."

I questioned if it's worth him going on this annual hiking trip, but he generally enjoys the companionship and the hiking, so he's chosen to adjust to changes in the behaviour of his old friends rather than swapping them for newer models.

Unless mental deterioration intervenes, we can retain control over matters like respect and good manners as we get older. Put bluntly, to be a friend, you've got to turn up. I have a friend who's always late. She knows it and has made New Year resolutions to be on time.

"I don't know why I do it," she intones.

She's been told, point-blank, that she's rude. Other friends just stop inviting her.

"But is punctuality really so important among friends?" Claire challenged.

Her friend, Nerida, thinks not. "Did I miss anything in that half-hour? You two weren't going anywhere. We're only catching up for a drink. You don't have to wait for me to get started. What's the problem?"

We all know them: The conscientiously correct, the righteous right, and those who have the strongest opinions in areas in which they have the least knowledge. Kathy's erstwhile friend, Marilyn, is one of these. Marilyn's a counsellor, so Kathy sought her advice about another friend, Suzanne, who was being bullied. Marilyn leapt to the conclusion that Suzanne must be mentally ill. To prove the point, she told Kathy to gather together a group of friends. She reckoned she'd be able to identify the one with mental health issues within minutes.

"As if I'm going to hold a party just so that she can play 'spot the lunatic'!" Kathy expostulated. For her, this friendship was over.

I've also got friends who want to be in 'the knowing position.' (That's not in the Kamasutra.) If I share my joy in a film, they've always seen it – usually twice and more than two years ago. Well, why didn't they say so instead of capping my stories?

I now block toxic people, including the one who launched an online character assassination of me in the guise of a book review. You've heard of BFFs. Well, I have FFs (Former Friends). Amy's an FF because I never knew what the next barb would be. When I proudly told her about the family history website I'd developed, she dismissed me, saying that she wouldn't give twenty cents to find out about her ancestry. She corrected me in front of others, and, when I asked her for editorial help with my writing, she replied, "What do you want me to do with this shite?" Perhaps you could shove it back where it came from, along with your friendship! This friendship has been culled.

Changing friendships in old age can mean the joy of new friends. Claire and I analysed this, noting the importance of propinquity and the fewer opportunities for it in retirement – unless we make things happen. Claire volunteered for a while: "It created a framework for forming friendships because we had regular opportunities to meet." This fits my understanding of friendship. I distinguish between groups of friends based on propinquity at different stages of my life: school friends, university friends, neighbourhood, and work friends. Some friendships have lasted. Others disappeared with propinquity.

I graduated from Liverpool University in 1970. We didn't have a reunion until 2010, which left me with the impression that we hadn't known much about each other as undergraduates. We'd aged and changed, so some were apprehensive about the reunion.

"I'm not certain about this," said one staunch defender of social justice. "I bet they all sent their kids to private school and vote Tory."

Not so! I was pleasantly surprised to discover that one old uni friend is the son of a leading trade unionist. I didn't know this at uni. I wish I had. We met as freshers and took off from there. Like the Little Prince in Saint-Exupéry's children's story, we left Planet Home and landed on Planet University, where we formed friendships and our new adult selves together. Then we graduated and left our friendships in their Liverpool home.

My annual expat Christmas letters, periodic return visits to the UK, and associated reunions may have cemented school friendships. If I'd stayed in England, we might have drifted apart. As one hometown school friend confided, she no longer had much in common with us. I understood because I've sometimes thought that, if we met now, we probably wouldn't become friends. We've walked very different paths in our adult lives. However, we didn't meet now, we met then, and, as Jacky said, our school is the knot that binds us together. They've certainly kept me connected with my youth, which balances how I've felt in Australia, where friends think I was born at the age of twenty-five when I migrated here.

Few in Australia are interested in my UK life, and I don't remember anybody in the UK asking about my life in Australia. They might get told, but they don't ask. Some years ago in Darwin, Geoff and I had an after-work drink before he headed back to England to see family.

"You know what it's like," he said. "When you get back, you're exotic for about five minutes because you live in Australia, but then it's back to local issues: 'Did you know there's a new bus stop at the end of our road?'" No, he didn't know.

There's a distinction between friends and acquaintances unappreciated by the wife in a cartoon I saw. Only one friend rocked up to her husband's funeral. "Strange!" she thought. "He had over a thousand friends on Facebook."

I was also misled about the distinction when I arrived in Australia because I saw the folk back 'home' in the UK as long-term 'friends' and the people I came to know and love in Australia as 'acquaintances' – short-term and en passant. It took me ages to realise that I'd known my Australian friends for longer, and better, than UK friends. My perceptions of friendship itself had to change.

As we've grown older, some friends have withdrawn from social life unintentionally. They've simply lost interest. I recently spent a day with an old friend – nice to see him, but not much fun. "In the book I wrote …" I started to say.

"I don't read anymore," he replied.

"When I was in Crete last year …" It transpired he doesn't travel anymore either. "I went to a great concert …"

This got a bite. He does listen to choral music, but mostly, he doesn't listen to music. I know not to impose my grandchildren on friends, but the occasional comical story is OK. So, I tried a few to jolly things along, but I came to appreciate that he doesn't like children. "In fact," he said, "I'm a bit of a recluse." He's let the old man in so there's a doubtful future in this friendship. I still wanna have fun.

Some old friends have intentionally withdrawn into themselves. They're reclusive by choice. One claims he doesn't have the emotional bandwidth to negotiate a social whirl. He just wants to meditate. Two friends are yoga teachers and spend a lot of time stretching, and another has joined his church, and wants to spend the rest of his life praying. They've changed. They're less into friendship now. They want a self-directed, quiet life, and if they can't do that in retirement, when can they? But what about me? I still want to know them.

Then there are the Eeyores. These friends haven't withdrawn from social life, but I wish they would. They cap every conversation with dire warnings of gloom and doom. "Are you travelling this Christmas?" he asked. So, I explained that I planned a classical music tour of Europe."What about COVID? It's still around – and flu. Did you say you'll be in London? There are train strikes, you know?" (Who didn't know that?) I wanted to ask what he thought about listening to music in the great opera houses of Europe – but I didn't.

You have to love Liverpool to get any sense of excitement about the moss-covered, dank, tunnelled rock walls that herald Lime Street Station, yet I savour the moment. This is my soul city. I look out for Phil, and there he is, just as he's always been for fifty years. Meeting me at the station is a ritual in our friendship. Now, in my seventies, I use Nordic Walking Poles when I travel. He's eighty-two and relies on a walking stick. So, when we met on a Lime Street platform last year, we started a sword fight with our mobility aids. I no longer stay at his place. It's a three-storey townhouse, and I can't cope with the steps, so I stay at a hotel that's a three-minute walk from the station. He really didn't need to meet me but he did because that's what these two old friends have always done. No changes needed here.

Lynne Hunt

Life on the slope in Liverpool

The 1707 Cotswold Farm

1940s Chic in Nuneaton

The end of the Nedlands House

Changing Places

I'm a bit of an expert on houses because I've lived in a lot of them. I attended eight different primary schools, and each meant a new house. Dad was a violent, drunken man so Mum had to strategise to keep a roof over the heads of her daughters. Born in 1910, she left school when she was thirteen. She had no qualifications but, as a Devonshire farmer's daughter, she could cook, and she did know how to raise and sell poultry. She consistently consulted 'The Lady' – a magazine in which the gentry advertised positions for live-in housekeepers and cooks. This was how she kept us from being homeless. But, with equal consistency, Dad undermined her efforts by quarrelling with the boss or drinking his grog. And so, we moved on. Change was my constant.

Mum actually owned the house into which I was born in 1948. It was probably bought with the money she inherited when her first husband died. The house was in Nuneaton – a UK coal mining town where Dad's family lived. It was a two-up-two-down worker's cottage with an outside toilet and no bathroom. Behind the back garden was a small field that Mum rented for the chicken coops in which she raised capons for local sale. I don't know how we all fitted into our house. At that stage, all four of Mum's girls lived at home. The eldest two shared one bedroom. Mum and Dad had the other, and sister number three was in a box room off their bedroom. As the youngest, my first bed was the bottom drawer of a chest of drawers.

One of the two downstairs rooms was given over to the young chicks that Mum bought to fatten up for quick sale. It had an oil heater to keep them warm. The other downstairs room was the living room, which had enough space in front of the fire for the tin bath used for Saturday night clean-ups. The tiled fireplace, bevelled edge mirror and sideboard, on which sat a wooden salad bowl and biscuit barrel, was quintessential 1940s chic. This room had to accommodate the dining table and chairs and an armchair for Dad. My memory must be wrong because I also remember a china cabinet. There couldn't possibly have been enough room for all this furniture and us – but it was there somewhere because Dad got drunk and kicked-in the china cabinet – Mum's treasured possession. He failed in the fruit and veg business that Mum established for him. So she sold the house, the older girls married, and sisters numbers three and four started on their trail of many houses. Each one told its own stories and provided a brick in the architecture of our lives.

Our first move was to Rugby, where we lived in the gatehouse to a local manor. Mum was the cook and Dad the butler. The house had a bath, which, surprisingly, was in the kitchen. It had a lid which served as a kitchen bench. I remember playing outside on the lawn with Janet, my new walkie-talkie doll, when I had my first encounter with a dragonfly. In fear, I flung Janet to the ground, thereby smashing her pottery head. I was devastated.

We lived in Rugby for only a few weeks before Dad got stuck into the boss' grog. It was such a short period of time that, but for Janet and the bath in the kitchen, I probably wouldn't even remember living there.

'The Lady' eventually led us to the Cotswolds and my all-time favourite honey-coloured limestone Cotswold farmhouse."We thought you protested too much," Ailsa said when we finally met. She now owns this house that still dominates my affections. It seems you can take the girl out of the Cotswold Farmhouse, but you can't take the Cotswold Farmhouse out of the girl. So, when I was newly retired and had time to fulfil some dreams, I decided I'd like to go back. I wrote a letter to the current owners, including photos of myself as a child at the farmhouse. I offered enough detail to avoid any suspicion that the letter might be a scam. It seems I overdid it, but they welcomed me graciously and friendship has grown from this first contact.

According to an inscription on a mantelpiece, this three-storey farmhouse was built around 1707. The attics at the top were filled with items left behind by aeons of tenants. It was a child's wonderland. I dressed up in camisoles and pantaloons that must have come from the early part of the twentieth century, if not before, and I played with the large collection of bird eggs I found there. It was a treasure trove! But my Cotswold wonderland must have been dreadful for Mum, who was allowed to live there rent-free if she fed the bullocks through winter. We had lots of rats and no running hot water, but we did have a bath – this time, actually in a bathroom. We had no electricity, no TV and no radio. I didn't miss them because I had the time and freedom to roam through fields and woodlands and to hear local stories that were tendrils to broader horizons.

Neighbouring Brough Wood, I was told, had been planted in memory of a local family's elder son killed in WWI. General 'Galloper Jack', a great friend of Winston Churchill, had family connections with Brough. The General wrote 'My Horse Warrior', which told the life story of his beloved horse, including leading the cavalry charge to halt the last major German offensive of the war in 1918. In 2014, on the anniversary of the start of WWI, Warrior was awarded the Honorary **PDSA** Dickin Medal on behalf of all animals that served in the First World War.

The contrast between the rural idyll of the Cotswolds and Liverpool, where I went to university, could not have been greater. Here, the rows of redbrick tenement houses told me different stories of the Industrial Revolution, dockland culture, edgy music, and comedy. I lived in Liverpool in the post-Beatles era, but their influence had remained. One of my student flats was immediately above the apartment belonging to the mother of Stuart Sutcliffe, the Beatle who died a young man's death in Hamburg. I know it's drawing a long bow, but I did feel as if I was living in the orbit of the Beatles.

We reckoned we could run pretty cheap student parties in one of my Liverpool share-houses because it was on a slope. One side of the house had collapsed into the sewer trench. We became accustomed to walking lopsided, but staggering party guests thought they'd drunk more than they could remember. I thought the house would have been demolished years ago, but, decades later, I returned to find it still standing. It was buttressed against the house next door, so I suppose it's a bit like teeth. Take one out, and you might wind up with a full set of dentures.

I backpacked to Western Australia in 1973 and soon discovered that it was cheaper to buy a house than to rent, especially when I was able to buy my first little weatherboard house in a beachside suburb for a mere AUS$12,000. At that stage, there were plans to widen the road in front of my house to four lanes. Beyond that lay the train line bordered by another four-lane highway. These plans made the location unattractive, so I sold and bought a house in Inglewood, near where I worked. I should have stayed near the beach. The road was never widened.

My Inglewood house was an attractive, tuck-pointed red brick home, well-located on a quarter-acre block near shops and restaurants. It had jarrah floorboards and leadlight windows. I loved that house, but I moved again in 1979 because marriage beckoned."Will you marry me? I'm ready for the renovations." Although my future husband thought he was understanding my needs, he actually wasn't because his words presumed that I would move in with him and his kids. In fact, we'd never discussed this.

"Why don't we get a bloody sky hook to hold up the roof whilst we demolish all the walls underneath?"

Clearly, my new husband wasn't as ready for the renovations as he'd thought.

"Righty-Ho," I replied and came close to doing just that. The trouble was that we didn't have enough money to move out, so the building happened around us. Each night, I cleared one end of the table of red dust so that we could eat meals cooked on a camping stove. There were no windows or doors in the front wall for many weeks.

"Yoo-hoo!" we heard one night as we ate our spagbol. She was stunned when she walked through the house and encountered us, forks suspended between plate and mouth. She'd thought the house was empty and barged in.

It transpired that this woman was the first to buy the house in 1932, and she was curious to see what was happening. She'd been a single mother who kept a roof over the heads of her kids by buying spec-built houses, doing them up and then selling at a profit. She and her children moved eight times in eight years. Years later, my daughter, Ruth, participated in a primary school oral history project. She and her classmates were invited into a nursing home to interview the elderly residents about their lives. Ruth interviewed a woman who'd also had to buy and sell houses to survive. I realised then that it was not an uncommon strategy for Australian women to eke out a living in this manner.

"Did you have a good life?" Ruth asked.

"No," replied her interviewee.

It was an awkward moment but an honest reflection on the difficulties of incessant house changes.

After fifteen years of married life, we relocated to Woodlands, which is close to the freeway and my new employment in the so-called new town of Joondalup. My husband found the Woodlands house and was surprised that I liked it because it was new. He knew that I'm a fan of jarrah floorboards and leadlight windows and these were not to be found in this house. But it had a separate wing of children's bedrooms, and our bedroom was on the top floor. It was just us! I'd helped to raise four stepkids, two of whom were live-in, and at this stage, I was raising our own two kids – soon to become teenagers. It had been a crowded marriage, and my husband and I would finally have our own space upstairs. What's not to like?

In 2023, my former Nedlands neighbour, Libby, started to send me daily photos to chart the demolition of my old house.

"Doesn't the demolition of your first married home upset you?" she asked.

I wasn't upset because I'd never liked it and it told me the story of my husband's first marriage – not mine. I'd had to accept living there because it was near my stepkids' schools. We could never have afforded to sell and buy back into Nedlands. In any case, I hadn't liked the house itself and I hadn't chosen it. Contrary to his philosophy of buying the worst house in the best street, my husband had bought the worst house in the worst street for $16,000 in 1969. It had no character and was on a busy road.

"But your kids were conceived there, and they grew up there," Libby persisted."Surely you must feel something about the demise of the house!"

I had to admit that it was a brick in the architecture of my life, but this house also told sad and dark stories, and it held secrets that I didn't discover until after my husband's death. I felt cleansed by the demolition.

Lynne Hunt

Twin Hearts

"What's the wool for Mum?" eight-year-old Ellen asked.

"I'm getting creative." Carrie lifted us from the bag and started sorting us into piles. "There are colours I'll never use," she grimaced before shoving me aside, "but the multi-pack was cheaper than individual balls."

I found myself at the bottom of the bag. From there, I watched as Carrie taught herself to crochet, slowly turning my fellow balls into artistic masterpieces. First, a long scarf, starting with messy loops and ending with neat stitches. Next came flowers.

When Carrie got bored of practising circles, she graduated to animals. An orange crab. A black penguin. An owl in two shades of purple. A green turtle. A blue rabbit. A yellow bee with striking black stripes.

She made each animal twice: a practice run, then the real deal.

Carrie crocheted until the bag sat empty, apart from leftover coloured strands. And me.

"Grey," she muttered, shaking her head.So drab." She rolled me in her palm. "Maybe ..."

Her eyes lit up. The needle flicked, her hands flew and suddenly I started taking shape. Stuffing made me plump and round. A scrap of pink wool became a nose and mouth; dark blue created eyes. Before I knew it, with a final stitch, I was complete.

"A cat!" Ellen exclaimed, then looked around. "Just one?"

Carrie shrugged. "He's bigger than I planned. There's not enough wool for another, so he'll have to do."

Despite her seeming indifference, I knew better. Carrie's joy in her work had infused every one of my fibres and filaments.

In her room, Ellen surveyed the bookshelf holding her new animal collection. "They all have twins." She shook her head as she looked at me. "You can keep me company. I don't have a twin either."

At bedtime, Carrie frowned and tried moving me to the shelf.

"No," Ellen was obstinate. "Twin stays here."

"You don't look anything like a cat." I heard Carrie's smile.

"We both have hearts," Ellen mumbled drowsily.

That night was the first of many spent squashed in Ellen's arms.

Some things endure.

The joy of laughter. The feel of tears soaking your wool. A cuddle's warmth. The stab of a needle when your ears are re-stitched or a frayed hole needs mending. The security of being wanted.

Other things mark time dissolving.

***

Conversation shifting from toys to parties. Eavesdropping when friends became Ellen's main confidants. Carrie's entire animal collection, except me, going to the op shop. Ellen's new room decor. The framed qualification. Travel photos displayed in albums. Boyfriends arriving and disappearing. Carrie frowning as she packed me into a box.

It was my turn to go.

I could see nothing. Just feel. The dark, uncertain silence. Bumpy jostling. Rumbling. Vibration. More jostling. A bruising thump as my box hit something hard. Scratching light as the lid opened.

"I have just the spot for you," said Ellen.

She placed me on a couch. In a living room. Ellen's living room. And later, Ellen and Alex's living room.

Carrie frowned when she saw me, but Ellen was obstinate. "Twin stays here."

Some things endure.

The joy of laughter. The feel of tears soaking your wool. A cuddle's warmth. The stab of a needle when your ears are re-stitched or a frayed hole needs mending. The security of being wanted.

Other things mark time dissolving.

A baby's cry. Being carted in a toddler's grubby fist. My move from the couch to Samantha's big-girl bed. Conversation shifting from toys to parties. Eavesdropping as friends became Samantha's main confidants. Samantha's new room decor. The framed qualification. Travel photos on a phone. Boyfriends arriving and disappearing. Unfathomable sadness when someone dies.

I realised what had happened when the tears soaking me were not Samantha's.

"I think she loved you secretly," Ellen whispered.

I smiled, remembering Carrie's satisfaction as she stitched.

At first glance, I might seem drab, but being a companion filled with life's memories … that's enough to make anyone shine.

Liz Hurst

A New Chapter in My Life

I have COVID-19 to thank for changing my life. I had it in December 2022, and while I was able to get antiviral medication, which limited my symptoms to just three days, I developed a really sore neck. It was caused by sleeping upright, so I didn't cough as much during the night. One evening, my support worker, Tracy, put me in my bath and massaged me with the excess shampoo bubbles. It felt ... nice. For the first time in my life I wondered if a special man would give me more opportunities to feel that way again.

When she put me to bed I told her how she made me feel. "Do you know there are disability sex workers?" Tracy asked. My mind boggled, especially when she said she used to be one!

The next day I worked from home and couldn't get the idea out of my head. After work I searched for 'male disability sex workers in Perth'. I had no luck until I realised they're known as escorts here. A website of independent escorts came up, and one in particular took my fancy. His profile said he was mid-30s, a straight male, and he listed 'disabled clients' as one of his services. But it was his smile that captured my heart. His name was Chayse.

A few days later I was sitting at home when I thought of him. Next thing I did was send him an email! Pre-COVID me would never have done that. I surprised myself by hitting Send. I included my phone number, and in less than ten minutes he called me.

I asked him practical questions, like does your house have wheelchair access? Could I stay in my chair for the massage? Where on the body do you start? Have you used a hoist before? My house or yours? He was patient and answered them all. He suggested I start with a two-hour erotic massage. I told him I'd think about it.

I had no clue at all when it comes to sexual matters. I was naive and ignorant. At 43 years old, I had never been kissed, nor had a boyfriend.

That night I told my support worker Kate what I had done. "Well, aren't you going to reply to him?" she asked. Before I knew it, I'd made an appointment for 22/1/23.

The next day I searched what to expect in an erotic massage. The results for women blew my mind. I couldn't stop reading. Most ended in a happy ending — was that what I thought it was? Could I achieve that? My excitement levels were so high that I had trouble sleeping and was so distracted at work that I kept making mistakes.

My appointment was still a month away. I would be an emotional wreck by then, so I changed it to 7 January. On Christmas Eve, Chayse video called me so I could see his place and ask another hundred questions. He was gorgeous and seemed genuine. I decided that if I was paying the same amount as every other woman, then I deserved the same treatment. Having the massage in my wheelchair would not be adequate.

In the week prior to my massage, I went to the dentist, got my eyelashes tinted, shaved my armpits for the first time in ages, plucked my old-lady chin hairs and tidied other hairy parts of my body. But some nerves and doubts started to dampen my excitement. Things like: is it safe? Is it legal? Could it be a scam? Will I like it? Will I like Chayse? This was the first time I'd be naked in front of a man outside a hospital — a huge step in a new chapter of my life. At least by paying for the service, I felt in control, despite surrendering my body to a man I hadn't met. It was in his best interest to make it a pleasant experience for me. A vulnerable situation to get myself into, but an exciting exploration of my body. A new year, and a new beginning, to really feel like a woman. Because COVID didn't kill me, I had a chance to try something new.

***

The day of my massage with Chayse finally arrived. I was still googling what to expect the night before and was surprised to learn that women masturbate. I thought it was something only men did. Did I mention that I knew nothing about sexual matters? We never spoke about it at home. My brothers got the usual sex talk: *don't get a girl pregnant before you're married, etc.* My parents didn't have to worry about me sneaking out in the middle of the night to sleep with a boy. There are some benefits to having a child with a disability.

I was at work the day before (don't know how I got any work done — my mind was distracted). My manager came to chat before she left."Any plans for the weekend?" she asked.

I gulped. *What do I tell her?* "I'm having a massage tomorrow," I said with a shaky voice.

"Ooh, how nice. A relaxing type of massage or physio style?"

"Definitely the relaxing type of massage," I replied, more confident this time.

She sounded excited for me."You'll have to tell me how it was next week."

Oh, no I don't think so, I thought.

An hour before my appointment we got my hoist in my van and left for Chayse's place. Half of me couldn't wait to get there. But the other half was like: *what have you got yourself into? Just stay home!*

I didn't listen to that voice though. Tracy and I had devised a plan that if either of us felt uncomfortable, we would ask for my blue water bottle, that we had left at home. She had also suggested that I write a list of things I was and wasn't comfortable with him doing to me, in a traffic light style. Green was yes please; orange was maybe — check with me before doing; and red was no thank you.

Being a secure apartment block, I called Chayse when we arrived. He came down to let us in and gave me a kiss on the cheek. He was taller and more handsome in real life. I was pleased he didn't kiss Tracy. One thing I hate is when people speak to my support worker instead of me. It was off to a good start and did a lot to ease my nerves.

Once in his apartment, he offered us water, and I noticed he had a snake enclosure. We chatted for a bit, but I was keen to start. After moving the massage table to the wall so I couldn't fall off, Tracy got me in the hoist. We'd planned to teach him how to use it, but he disappeared.

"Oh, I thought I'd give you some privacy," he said when I called him over.

I laughed. "When you're about to do what to me?"

"Fair enough."

As Tracy got me on the table, I suggested he read my list. I'd given him an envelope containing it and the cash. It also had things in it that I wasn't comfortable saying out loud, especially with Tracy in the room.

He finished reading as Tracy moved my chair out of the massage room. I assured her that she was safe to leave, but the plan was for her to stay close for the first 30 minutes, just in case we needed her.

Chayse entered the room and closed the double doors. The room had no window, so was softly lit by a lamp in the corner. He removed his shoes and socks, then his shirt and finally his shorts. All of a sudden I felt hot!

"How are you feeling?" he whispered as he got some warm massage oil on his hands.

"A bit scared," I said. He came over and rubbed my leg. "I'm scared of two things," I confessed. "One is falling asleep." After weeks of excitement and not sleeping well, the last thing I wanted was to nap during the massage. I'm glad he didn't ask what the second thing was — it was farting!

He tugged at my dress. "How do we get this off you?" he asked.

"Just pull," I said. I was wearing a purple silk dress that was gathered around my upper body. It had no sleeves, and I chose it as was easy to get on and off, and I didn't need a bra. He was really gentle and placed it on a chair nearby. My knickers came off just as easily.

I was naked on the table; in front of a man I had just met. I took a deep breath as he rubbed oil along my legs.

He usually starts with the woman face down on the table. But I'd told him that wasn't possible for me. We compromised, and he rolled me on to my side, facing the wall.

Chayse continued to rub oil over my body in long continuous strokes. At times he dripped it on to me then rubbed it in. I enjoyed his touch. But after a few long strokes down my leg, causing it to spasm, I had to ask him to place a cushion between the wall and my knee. His strokes were pushing my knee into the wall, making it hurt. Not long after, my arm went to sleep, and I had to ask him to move it out from under me. There's nothing like pain and discomfort to kill the mood.

He gave me a lovely foot massage and I closed my eyes. When he finished, he asked, "Are you asleep?"

"No," I replied. I'd actually been wondering when he was going to get more personal. I didn't have to wait much longer.

He rolled me back over and started massaging my upper body. As he got closer and closer to my breasts with his left hand, his right hand was getting further up my legs. It was gradual and I felt comfortable with him touching me there. His breathing pattern changed, and he was making a few deep grunts.

The next thing he did surprised me. He leant over and sucked my left nipple while his fingers went to town below. I found it weird and felt no arousal whatsoever.

After what felt like ages, he stood up, with a look of disappointment on his face. *Was I supposed to have felt something?* I felt bad for him.

"I do have a vibrator," he said.

"Is that included in the massage?" I asked. Sex toys were on my list in the orange section. I was curious to know what they looked and felt like.

"It can be," he said with a smile on his face. He turned away and opened a drawer. When he showed me the device, I was shocked.

"Does that go ... inside me?" It was an enormous black contraption. The length was as long as his forearm, with a ribbed ball on the end. The ball was probably larger than a tennis ball.

"No," he laughed."This is an external vibrator."

Phew! He plugged it in and turned it on. I held out my hand so I could feel it. It was on the lowest setting, and didn't seem too scary. "Ok, let's try."

He started it, and it was quite pleasant. My legs were spasming a lot, but I noticed my breathing pattern had changed. I was taking much deeper breaths. He asked if he should turn it up and I said yes, a little.

I was starting to enjoy it, when all of a sudden I got a headache and I had to ask him to stop. It felt like the top of my head was about to explode.

"Is this normal?" I asked.

Chayse shook his head and told me he'd had 100% success rate with the device — until me.

Oops. Why me? It wasn't for his lack of effort that things weren't going well. We chatted for a few minutes and my headache went away.

I asked him what the time was.

"20 minutes left," he replied.

"Is that all?" I asked. "Shouldn't I be getting dressed soon?"

"Na, plenty of time." So he switched on the vibrator again, but within a minute or two my headache returned, and we had to stop.

Chayse put it away, wiped his hands clean and picked up my knickers. "How do I put these on you?" he asked.

I laughed. I guess he hasn't had to help many women get dressed. "Just make sure they're right way and not inside out, and you'll be fine," I said.

He managed to pull them up pretty well, and my dress too. At least I was decent enough to go home. Chayse reckoned he could lift me back into my wheelchair, so he went and got it from the other room.

The transfer was successful, but only just. My bum landed on the front of the seat, and as I was wearing a silk dress, was at risk of sliding off. "It's time you called Tracy," I said. He had to stand with his knees against mine to stop me sliding off, but managed to reach his phone and called her.

Remember, at this point Chayse is still only wearing his briefs. And now they're at my eye-level. *Only fair since he's seen me naked.*

While on the phone I had an idea. By the time he'd finished, I'd tilted my chair back. All he had to do was push my knees and I slid right back. Tracy came in (Chayse had given her his keys so she could swipe her way back in again) and was shocked to see me in my chair.

"You're up and dressed!" Tracy said.

She only had to get me a bit more comfortable. Moving my legs or touching my feet always makes me spasm, especially when I'm not wearing shoes. I got Tracy to show Chayse how to stop the spasm by pressing my magic 'buttons' — applying pressure to my knee.

"Wow, when did you have the buttons installed?" he asked in a serious tone.

We laughed so much. *Did he really think that I'd had surgery to install buttons in my legs?* It was a great leveller. What I didn't know about sex, he didn't know about disability. We had plenty to teach each other.

Before Tracy arrived, I'd been telling Chayse about my other fantasies. One was for him to give me a bath. "I have a spa bath," he said. I love my bath, but adding jets is like heaven to me. I asked him to show me before we left. It was big and deep. I would have given anything to jump in right then. I told Chayse I'd think about it. But I knew there wouldn't be a safe way of putting me in his bath or getting me out. It's times like these that I wish I wasn't disabled. I would have to find another way to enjoy a spa together, and safely.

I reversed my chair out of the passageway. There were two bedrooms on my right. One was very messy, and the other was neat and tidy.

"You've got two bedrooms?" I remarked, looking at the clean bed.

"Yeah, that's the work bed," he said.

The work bed? There wouldn't be many people who can say they have one at their house. A good reminder that this is his job. Chayse devoted the last two hours to me and my body, but he will do the same thing to the next woman who walks through his door.

On that note, we left, promising to email him tomorrow. He kissed me on the cheek as we said, "See you soon."

***

Over the next few months, Chayse helped me cross every item off my fantasy list. His guidance and exploration of my body resulted in a confidence I'd never experienced. I could see myself as a woman first, with the same needs, dreams and desires as any other. Yes, my disability made some things tricky, but we worked out what we could enjoy together.

Today I am living a dream: my first boyfriend James moved into my place at the end of 2024. It's a surreal feeling waking up next to the man I love every day. We're great friends and he's an excellent lover. I can't believe how lucky I was to get COVID, have that conversation with Tracy that led me to my first lover, and now my first love. It certainly changed my life.

Melanie Hawkes

Winning Entry – 2025 Jennifer Burbidge Short Story Award.

The Stick that Changed my Life

The elevator doors closed behind me, but it didn't move.

Uh-oh, I thought. *Now what?*

In the 14 years I'd been a wheelchair user, I'd never been in a lift on my own before. But here I was, in my first semester of a Japanese Studies degree at Murdoch University, and needing to get to the second floor for a lecture on cross-cultural psychology. It was a very small lift in an old building at the opposite end to the lecture room. My arms weren't long or straight enough to press the button to go up. I was stuck. For about an hour. And missed my lecture.

This was 1997, before everyone had a mobile phone, so I couldn't even call for help. Eventually, someone came to use the lift and found me – what a surprise they got. I was just relieved to be out of there. Lucky I don't get claustrophobic.

That afternoon when my mum came to pick me up, I told her what had happened. "You need to carry a stick," she said.

Being the practical person Mum is, we stopped at Bunnings on the way home. She bought me a wooden dowel, a pack of rubber stoppers that fit the end, and some plastic tubing. When we got home, she put a rubber stopper on one end of the dowel, cut some tubing and slid it over the other end, and gave it to me. Voila: my stick was born.

I put the plastic tubing end into my mouth and tested my stick on a light switch. Oh my goodness, it worked! For the first time in my 17 years, I could do things I'd never thought possible, like turn a light on or off. This would be the start of the independent life I'd craved. Thanks, Mum!

But what else could I use it for? I looked around my room. If I hooked the little rubber stopper on my pencil tin on my desk, I – oh yes – I could bring it closer or push it out of my way. I learnt that I could also scratch my head, type on my computer and open and close doors. While I was living with my parents and three younger brothers, it hadn't occurred to me that I'd need to be capable of doing these things for myself if I wanted to move out of home and not need 24-hour care.

The only challenge with my new stick was how to carry it? I'd need it at uni to press lift buttons, so I wouldn't get stuck ever again. My stick might be small in diameter but was about a metre long. It was too big to carry on my tray.

My dad got to work in his shed. He was a boilermaker and had lots of tools at home. It didn't take him long to develop a stick holder. Made from aluminium tubing, he blocked the bottom, and attached a bracket to screw to my leg rest. I now had a stick and could carry it everywhere I went. Thanks, Dad!

I developed an independent spirit from that day. My parents had always encouraged me to do as much as I could for myself, while accepting help for the things I couldn't. But with this stick, I could demonstrate it practically to others. I'm certain it helped me be accepted as an exchange student to Japan in 1999 for 10 months. I wasn't taking no for an answer and was determined to fulfil my university studies degree by studying at a Japanese university.

**

The problem with wooden sticks is they broke often. And when overseas studying, it became an issue. We found a hardware/garden centre that had my stick replaced quickly, every time I broke it.

Once back in Perth, I graduated and had to find a job. I was invited to be a guest speaker at disability awareness training sessions for Main Roads staff. I always started my talk by showing my stick and asking what people thought it helps me with.

After one presentation, a man at the back put his hand up to ask me a question. "Why do you use a wooden stick? Have you ever used fibreglass sticks?"

I shook my head. During the morning tea break we chatted further. "We use them as flag poles for the orange flags at children's school crossings," he explained. "We often get them back a bit worn out. I could deliver some to you next week."

Sure enough, the following week he delivered four to my door. They were slightly slimmer than the wooden ones I was used to, and a little heavier. I had to build my jaw muscles to be able to use it effectively, since I use it in my mouth for most things. It took me a while to get used to it, but I haven't broken a stick since. I'm still using the original ones – for over 20 years now.

In 2015, I received my third assistance dog, Upton. He found my stick difficult to pick up off the floor. He couldn't get his front teeth underneath it. "What if we added an elastic band?" his trainer asked me.

With the band in place, Upton learnt to target the band to pick it up every time. But I quickly found another use for it: tagging my Smartrider card on and off buses and trains. I always carried my card in a plastic pouch with a pipe cleaner handle, and dangled it from the end of my stick. But on buses, the tag-on machine is above my head height, so the pouch always slid and hit me in the face. The elastic band stops it sliding, and since then I haven't had to ask other passengers to tag on for me. Thanks, Upton!

In 2023, I was browsing social media when I saw a competition called the Simply Open Awards. They were looking for simple solutions and innovations that can help people with disabilities. I made a five-minute video about my stick. I explained why I needed it, how it was made, and demonstrated several uses around my home, from pressing light switches to sliding doors open and closed. I even showed how I can heat my leftover dinner in the microwave with the short stick I have.

One evening I received an email saying I was a prize-winner (a cash prize of £750), and my video had been sent to the judges at the Discovery Awards. The next night I received an email saying my video was voted the top two innovations IN THE WORLD, and my prize was a trip to Vienna to attend the Zero Project Conference in February 2024! All because of the video I made about my stick. The stick I carry everywhere because I was stuck in a lift and couldn't reach the button. The same stick that has enabled me to catch public transport to work independently, and not need 24-hour care. It really did change my life.

Melanie Hawkes

A Brand New Light

(Pop Song Lyrics)

In the quiet of the night, when the stars shine bright,
We waited, hand in hand, dreaming of this moment, so divine.
With a gentle cry, you arrived, our hearts opened wide,
A miracle in our arms, our love's sweetest sign.

(Chorus)
Oh, welcome to the world, little one,
You're the laughter, you're the fun.
With every smile, you'll show us grace,
In your eyes, we see our place.
You're a brand new light, guiding our way,
Our hearts are forever changed today.

Tiny fingers wrapped 'round ours, this love feels like a dream,
You've painted our lives in colours you've never seen.
From your first breath to your first steps, every moment so dear,
We promise to protect you, always keep you near.

(Chorus)
Oh, welcome to the world, little one,
You're the laughter, you're the fun.
With every smile, you'll show us grace,
In your eyes, we see our place.
You're a brand new light, guiding our way,
Our hearts are forever changed today.

(Bridge)
Sleepless nights and joyful days,
We'll treasure each and every way,
You've opened our hearts, made us whole,
You've written a story deep in our soul.

(Chorus)
Oh, welcome to the world, little one,
You're the laughter, you're the fun.
With every smile, you'll show us grace,
In your eyes, we see our place.
You're a brand new light, guiding our way,
Our hearts are forever changed today.

(Outro)
So here's to new beginnings, to laughter and to tears,
You've brought us so much joy that will last through the years.
As we hold you close, never let you go,
In this world, little one, we promise you'll always know,
You're our brand new light, and forever you'll stay,
In our hearts and memories, come what may.

Helen Iles

Available on Spotify and other online music platforms on 'The Gravity of Us' album on The Sound of Poetry *record label in August 2025*

A Change of Heart

Beebus scurried through the underbrush on all fours, careful not to snap or crack a branch in his haste. He folded his long gold ears forward and around his face, fluted them to channel scent and sound to his snout and auditory channels; sucked in his gross rotundness so it wouldn't scrape along the ground and leave a trail. He knew the fine pinpricks of his digits would leave a minor trace of his travels, but not one so obvious as the bow wave his belly would leave.

He headed in the general direction of the river, for riders scoured the hills, and Chomwits hated water so they would ne'er search for him there. He moved with caution, his long tufted tail tucked in tight so not to be the usual signal beacon it was. Equally, the high coif of his shaggy strip-mane was pressed flat by his frilled ears, further hiding his movements.

"Go quietly, Beebus. Make nerry a sound less the Saurills find you. You not be nice tasting fodder in their evil black mouths." He chanted the words to keep his fear down, but the image only made him more fearful. He hoped Glimlick had made it to safety – splitting up had been the only way to foil them.

"And what when you reach the river?" The question reeled in his mind; poured out through violet lips."You be at the water then."

He honestly hadn't thought of that before. What would he do when he reached the water?

"You go down river. Find the bridge," he said to himself. "Get help for Glimlick."

His courage rose with his plan. "Cast a full-on Chomwit assault on the Saurillons." He laughed openly at the thought, then said: "Nope. Nope, nope, nope. Would never do." Chomwits didn't like to fight.

He noticed the brush was starting to thin, plucked his feet more subtly from the ground, and made more stealth. The scrub soon opened to a clearing, and he lifted his blunt, snubby snout to the air and sucked in the surroundings. He noted the subtle hints of lavender and aromatic primrose; a briny patch of earth an Alker had piddled on; the putrid remains of long-dead carrion way to the north, and, he shivered, water. No bitter scent of Saurillon. No nasty little pocket of acridity that wrinkled his nose and made his skin turn yellow. He felt safe. Felt very safe. And so, keeping his golden eye on the tumbling stream, he stepped out onto green, and rose to his full potential – a Chomwit four foot high, now with blue-tinged skin given his prowess at outwitting his enemy.

He withheld the cackle this time, for he still had to reach the bridge, still had to formulate a plan better than a full-on assault.

He turned downstream, and the blueness of his coat poured down into the points of his needle-like toes and faded into oblivion. He now stood a ghastly shade of lemon with an orange-tufted tail and mane strip, and bright golden ears. The ears now pinned back against his head, hugged each other tightly, for straight in front of him, a short way across the clearing, stood the Saurillon, Glimlick suspended by his scruff from the evil one's claw.

Beebus shivered, but the palid shade did not withdraw, and he literally stood and shook in his bootless feet.

"Come, Chomwit. Come and save your raggedy little friend." The voice was depthless, seemed to come from the pit of the creature's stomach as it shook Glimlick roughly in the air.

Beebus hoisted his huge paunch from in front of him, stuffed it higher upon his person, pushed it away into his not-too-far-away armpits.

The Saurillon stood firm, his pitch-black outfit hugging his bulging thighs and broad, powerful musculature. The breeze ruffled its three-quarter cloak and the shock of bright red feathers that streaked the centre-line of its brow and all the way over its crown and down its neck. Its red slitted reptilian eyes bore down on Beebus, who had only one thought in mind. "Run, Beebus. You are no match for Saurillon. Run. Run. Run," he urged himself.

The Saurillon laughed again; laughed loudly.

Beebus's ears suddenly pricked forward, their erectness doubling his width. "Must run. Must run," he said again. "No, no, no. Must save Glimlick."

His words prompted the Saurillon to draw the broad silver sword from its belt in readiness.

"Shut my mouth," Beebus said. "Attack now. Save Glimlick."

Again, the Saurillon laughed. A Chomwit against an armed Saurillon was ludicrous!

Nevertheless, Beebus slapped himself three times in the forehead, and his yellow pallor again began to hint at blue. His paunch plopped to the ground again, hit the earth with a thud and rebounded back into place.

The Saurillon cut the air three times with his blade, proving readiness; it shot a glance sideways at Glimlick as he also slapped himself three times in the forehead with the heel of his hand. The movement brought caution to its slitted eyes.

Beebus moved, pulled his ears frantically, down down, down down down. So did Glimlick.

Beebus's spindly legs extended downwards, pushing his height upward, stretching the burdensome belly to its fullness – pumped muscle. Then he tweaked his cheeks and a horrendous set of fangs protruded swiftly upward and downward from his jaw, like steel daggers. He snapped them together twice, loud clashes ringing across the space between them. Saliva dripped groundward from peeled-back lips.

The threat in the Saurillon's eyes changed, a flicker of apprehension appearing to lower the sword.

"Oh ho," he said in gravelly tones as Glimlick tweaked his cheeks."A changling, no doubt."

"Oh ho," Beebus the Terrible mimicked him."Can't hide in the bushes when you're seven feet tall."

The black rider looked more wary, shot a glance sideways as Glimlick sneered and snapped off his head in one steely bite, snuffing his existence in a second. He landed on the earth with a plop as the Saurillon crumpled.

Moving forward, Beebus gave him a high five and moved off towards the bridge, their paunches drooping slowly, their colour returning to shades of green and mauves, their orange tufted signal beacons waving nonchalantly in the breeze as they walked.

"I do so hate violence," Beebus said whimsically.

"So do I. So do I," his friend replied, pushing a razor-sharp point back into concealment with a finger.

Helen Iles

At Season's Break

Ah, the sound of rain on a leaky tin roof, the smell of wet hay and damp grass, and rain ... Did you know you can smell rain? It has this refreshing smell before it even lands on your shoulder, before it mixes with the ground and turns the dust to mud, a smell of hope that washes the long summer problems away.

I breathe it in deeply, savour it, let it soothe my senses. Within a week, the brown earth will be green again, the patches of grass in the holding yards we have managed to sustain for ailing stock will be lush and clean, renewed. I stand inside the stable doorway, watch the spattering large drops form puddles – the ground cannot drink it fast enough – and wonder whether to turn the horses out, or leave them in. I turn, debating. Just how much drier is it in here than out there – we didn't get the roof fixed again this year ...

Jeremiah is watching the droplets fall from the bush timber beams into the corridor, his big grey head lifting and following the next drops down like a vertical game of tennis. It keeps him occupied. Across from him, Silver's long shaggy mane catches more drops and he shakes his massive head, dispelling most of it. He would prefer to stay in today – at least until the worst of the first downpour is over. My gaze runs over the length of the roof, checking that no major torrents are falling inside the stalls. And breathe with relief – most holes are along the corridor, from corrosion along the ridge-capping and from nails that have popped up in the strong easterly winds – fixable if someone was around to assist me in climbing on the high-pitched roof and re-nail the corrugated iron to the timbers. It would have to happen soon.

More heads appear over doors. The nickering starts. It's breakfast time and I duck into the feed shed and start pouring grain and chaff into buckets, each bucket receiving its special ingredient – sunflower seeds for Jeremiah, maize for Irish, sand lube for the ponies. Carrots all round. A loud rumble of thunder accompanies the pouring of grain and pony cubes. When the munching starts, I know they will prefer to be inside today. Me too.

Helen Iles

Stand Up

(Rock Song Lyrics)

The skies were blue, the water's clean,
Now we watch the fading green,
Ice caps melting, forests burning,
We're caught in a cycle, the world is turning.

(Chorus)
Hear the call of the future, it's ringing loud,
We can't ignore it, we must stand proud,
To stand for the earth, for the air we share,
To fight for our kids, to show that we care.

The earth is scorched to where ocean lies,
And storms rage worse; there's no disguise,
Our children's faces show worry and fear,
It's time to act; the message is clear.

(Chorus)
Hear the call of the future, it's ringing loud,
We can't ignore it, we must stand proud,
To stand for the earth, for the air we share,
To fight for our kids, to show that we care.

(Bridge)
We need to pull our heads from the sand,
Heed the signs and not pretend,
Let's harness the sun and the wind, take action,
stand up against our planet's destruction.

Plant the seeds of change, let them grow,
Innovate, collaborate, let commonsense flow,
Each small action … a ripple in the water,
Do it for the future of our sons and our daughters.

(Chorus)
Hear the call of the future, it's ringing loud,
We can't ignore it, we must stand proud,
To stand for the earth, for the air we share,
To fight for our kids, to show that we care.

(Outo)
So let's start today, hear the earth's soft plea,
For a world that will thrive, where all can be free.
With every heartbeat, each breath that we take,
We'll build a better climate, for our children's sake.

Let's save the planet so the land will heal
You have to believe that climate change is real
Ice caps are melting, forests are burning,
We're caught in a cycle, and the world is … dying.

Helen Iles

To be released on Spotify on The Sound of Poetry *record label in early 2026*

Who's Coming to Tea?

Lilian

They are playing so nicely. Claire throws the ball to Rob and Rob throws it back. They are lovely children. Everyone says I'm lucky to have children who play together without quarrelling. It will be time to go home soon. I'll give them another five minutes and then I'll call them.

Who's that woman going up to them? She's taking them away with her.

'Help, help! My children are being kidnapped.'

Everyone's looking at me and the woman and Claire and Rob have stopped and turned around. A crowd is gathering and this kind young man is looking concerned. He's asking if I'm all right. 'No, I'm not all right. That woman is taking my children away.'

There's a woman hurrying towards me with ice-cream cones in her hand. She's shouting something. I recognise her. I've seen her somewhere before. She's my friend.

Claire

I only left Mum for ten minutes to buy ice creams and it happened again. She mistook two children for Rob and me. She lives in the past. The doctor said I shouldn't worry and I shouldn't contradict her.

'She's happy in the past,' he said. 'Let her be there.'

That's all well and good, but not when she threatens to kidnap other people's children. She forgot all about it when she saw the strawberry ice cream, her favourite.

I love my mum. She doesn't know who I am most of the time. It makes me sad to see her like this.

She likes the beach. She's asking me to take off her sandals so we can wade at the water's edge.

Lilian

I love the feel of the sand between my toes, but why haven't we brought Jake? He enjoys running along the beach and dashing into the water to retrieve his ball.

My friend has gone all teary and takes my hand and says Jake was a beautiful dog. I guess he's staying home with Harry, my husband.

I haven't seen my mother and father for a while. They live close to the beach and I think we should drop by. My friend shakes her head and says they won't be there today. She says her name is Claire. What a coincidence! I ask if we can go another day. We should take Claire and Rob with us. I'm worried about them. Where have they gone?

Claire

Dad died eight years ago and Mum talks about him as if he's still here. It's unnerving. I'm not sure I can keep doing this. Mum has gone downhill since she's been in the care home. Rob said we had to do it; that we had to place her in care. I'm still not sure it was the right thing.

Can you imagine? Mum is eighty-six and worries about her parents! Alas, they are long gone.

Rob can't cope and rarely visits.

The home is doing a barbecue lunch today, with close relatives welcome. I'll stay with Mum to ensure she eats something. There aren't enough staff in the dementia unit. They are kind and caring, especially Maria, but always busy and overworked.

Lilian

This hotel is familiar. I've been here before. I'm staying the night and then I'm going home.

It's a barbecue today. I love barbecues. My friend says Harry can't join us. That's a shame. He likes to put on his striped apron. It makes him look like a butcher.

I'm enjoying my sausage in a bun. There's ice cream for dessert, but no strawberry, only vanilla. You'd think a hotel could do better than that. I'll complain.

My friend has disappeared so I ask why my children aren't here. All children love a barbecue. A woman, who says her name is Maria, sits me down with a cup of tea and says Claire visits nearly every day and often takes me out. That's nonsense. How could a little girl drive a car and take me out?

And what about Harry; why isn't he here? Maria asks if I remember the car accident. I don't know what she's talking about. She says a lot of things that don't make sense. I don't want to stay here.

Some of these people are weird. They walk about aimlessly, like robots. Maria says I'm safe here, but I know I'm not. Visitors come and go as they please. They tap that gadget with the numbers and the door opens for them. I've tapped it but nothing happens.

The barbecue is over and I've put on my hat. It's new. I like it. I'm wearing my sunglasses and my handbag is on my arm and I'm in the middle of a group of visitors. One of them taps away and the door opens. They're chatting to each other and don't notice me. I follow them as they know the way out.

They've got into their cars and driven away, but I'm heading for the street. I know this street. I've walked here often. I can see the deli with the bus stop opposite. My house is around the next corner.

Claire

The Care Home has called to say Mum has disappeared. She's missing. They can't find her. That's impossible. She must be somewhere in the unit. It's shaped like a horseshoe with an entrance each end. There's a keypad to enter and exit. Mum doesn't know how to use a keypad. We gave up on her mobile phone years ago. She couldn't use the numbers in sequence when we wrote them down for her.

The community rooms are in the centre of the horseshoe – the dining room, TV lounge, quiet room, activity room and so on. The bedrooms, each with its ensuite, are on the outer edge. Mum must be in one of them, possibly in a bathroom. If not, I'll call the police.

Lilian

My house key isn't in my bag. I'll have to ring the doorbell. Harry may be back from work by now.

A strange woman answers the door. I don't understand. I didn't invite her. 'Who are you? What are you doing in my house?' I ask.

She doesn't answer but half closes the door and calls for someone called Art.

Art opens the door wide and nods when I say it's my house. He invites me in and helps me up the step. I glare at the woman and stay close to Art.

They've changed my kitchen. It's all white with a silver-coloured fridge and dishwasher. That's good. I've always wanted a dishwasher but Harry says it isn't necessary.

I ask them if Harry is home yet. The woman smiles but doesn't answer. She's made me a cup of tea and gives me a slice of her home-made cake. Maybe she's not that bad, after all. Except she hasn't explained why she's in my house or why Harry isn't here. I don't remember inviting her.

Art has been making a phone call. I like him. He can stay – at least until Harry gets back.

There goes the doorbell. Harry has forgotten his key again.

No, it's that kind lady, I'm not sure who she is. I think she's my friend. I invite her to sit down and have a cup of tea. And, yes please, I'll have another piece of cake. I'll slip another slice in my handbag for later.

My friend thanks Art and the woman and says they have done wonders with the kitchen.

She says we have to go and she's sorry for something or other. I'd like to take the pretty teacup with me, but she says I have to leave it here. I'm not sure who she is. She reminds me of someone.

Claire

I'm angry with Maria and the other staff. How could they have let Mum escape? Oh dear, what a terrible thing to say – that she needed to escape, to want freedom. Somehow Mum found our old house. She'd lived there nearly sixty years. Rob and I were brought up there. Our children often stayed overnight with Nana and Pops.

Mum's dementia started before Dad's car accident, but it got noticeably worse after. She'd been able to manage with Dad caring for her. Rob and I tried to keep her in the old house with regular carer visits and days out with a local aged organisation. I filled the gaps myself, visiting frequently, but it wasn't enough. It became unsafe for her to be left alone, even for a short time.

It's bizarre that she has forgotten so much and yet remembers the house and the distant past.

Lilian

I'm back at the hotel and it's time for dinner. I'm staying the night. My friend has gone away. She said something about having to cook dinner for her family. She reminds me of someone. I wonder where Claire and Rob are? Harry must be looking after them.

I didn't like the fish and chips tonight. I wasn't hungry but I enjoyed the jelly and custard for dessert. I'm looking for the room with the TV set. It's here somewhere. I must ask if anyone has seen my mother and father. I haven't seen them for a while.

Here comes that man again. He always wears his hat, even indoors. He thinks he's a cowboy. He likes to pinch my arm or my bottom as he goes past. What's he doing? He's squeezing my breast and it hurts. He won't stop. He says Harry is dead. 'Help! Help me someone!'

A woman has come running and she's calling for help. It's taken three people to get him away from me. He's still yelling and shouting and saying nasty things. At last he's gone quiet. I think he's asleep. Two men have carried him away on a stretcher. I hope he never comes back.

The doctor has come to see me. He makes me undress. I don't want to. A woman called Maria helps me. She says Claire will be here soon. What use a little girl will be, I don't know.

Claire

I've been called back to the home. This is the worst Saturday of my life. A resident has assaulted Mum. How could that happen? The police have been called and Mum is receiving medical attention. This is too much. I'm not sure I can cope much longer. Mum doesn't even recognise me. I wish Rob would help more.

Thank goodness Mum isn't seriously hurt. The doctor said bruising and soreness of the breast. At least she doesn't need to go to hospital. She'd find it confusing.

Her assailant has been sedated and taken away . He'll not be allowed back in the dementia unit.

Maria has asked if I can stay with Mum until she settles. Poor Maria. Her shift should have ended two hours ago. I guess she's under stress and her family suffers too.

Lilian

My friend has turned up again. She's with two important-looking people. The man's wearing a business suit. He keeps looking round and wrinkling his nose as if there's a bad smell. The lady looks smart too, but she has a kind face and asks her questions nicely. She asks about the man. What man? Of course I'm all right. I ask if they've seen my mother and father.

It's supper time already. I'm having a cup of cocoa and a digestive biscuit. I have to take a tablet. I don't want to. I think they're trying to drug me. My friend says it will help me sleep and I need that tonight. She talks about the man again. What man?

If I can't sleep, I'll get up and walk around. I've always done that. Sometimes Harry joins me and we make a pot of tea and watch a film on TV. Harry says I'll be all right because he's here to care for me. He's not home yet. He must be working late. I hope he hasn't left me for another woman. He smiles too much at that woman in the library.

I haven't swallowed the tablet. It's in a corner of my cheek. When no one's looking, I'll spit it out. Harry will be here soon. I wonder if he'll call in on the way to see my mother and father. They're looking after Claire and Rob.

My friend is bringing me a cup of tea in bed. She reminds me of someone. She says her name is Claire. What a coincidence! There's something about Harry I should remember. I know it's not a good thing, but I wish I could remember.

Drat! I've swallowed the pill with my tea. I'm going home tomorrow. Harry, Claire and Rob will be there. I miss them so much. I'm feeling sleepy. Perhaps we'll have visitors again for afternoon tea.

Jean Alice Jenkins

Time to Say Goodbye

"You don't like change, do you? It will be your undoing."

Confronting words from a former employer. They were insulting. I swallowed a sharp response. Change is inevitable. From the moment we are born, change is unavoidable. The world evolves through change. From childhood, through adolescence, the blossoming of a woman's body into adulthood, marriage, children and so on…What a silly comment!

I never gave it much thought. Life is too short to worry about the little things. Those provocative comments now ran around my head. But what about the big things? I am now facing the most significant challenge of my 79 years. Massive life changes that will define me forever. How can I go on without him? My soul mate, my friend, my lover…my husband? I brush away the tears, turning to the sounds across the room, reminding me I am not alone.

Gathering my dignity, I watch the workers remove the hospital-designed furniture installed to nurse my sick husband. Despite its size, the custom-made bed provided comfort in those final, terrible months. They remove the over-the-bed table, pushing it aside to pack the medical equipment to monitor his blood pressure and heart rate. Unused medication fills the bins, a stark reminder of a difficult period in our long and mostly happy marriage.

Consumed with a deep sadness, I remove the spent flowers, a symbol of caring, from so many friends. His books, a mobile phone, and an empty glass are poignant reminders of his illness. I will leave them for the moment.

Philip hated hospitals. I couldn't blame him. The rigid routine and chaotic management provided little comfort to a sick man. Trailed by their eager students, doctors' rounds brought an air of indifference, the master performing for his audience. I wondered if they remembered that a patient was a human needing sensitive care and healing, not simply a body to be prodded, tested, and studied? There was no emotional attachment; the puppets were going about their business. A few minutes here, then they were gone.

A curtain separated the beds in his two-bed ward. Sounds from across the room constantly reminded us we were not alone. There was no privacy—only the distress of someone else needing care.

It was a conundrum. How did you get a straight answer when your heart told you your beloved was critically ill? Staff changeovers and the all-consuming talkfests demanded my presence at his bedside throughout the long day, monitoring his care. Staff shortages, a desperately challenged hospital system and a shortage of private rooms prompted my decision to nurse Philip at home. I questioned the cost of private health cover. It was a challenge. A private hospital or a government hospital? There was little difference, and switching between them proved costly.

Medical appointments, hospital visits, and a thinly held optimism that Philip would recover consumed our lives. It is no secret that our health system is in trouble, and the hospitals aren't coping. People with minor complaints cram the already overloaded emergency rooms in every hospital. The masses blame COVID for this health care crisis. However, we believed it was an incompetent government that was more concerned with winning votes than looking at the actual problems.

Finally, tired and dispirited, I had had enough. It wasn't easy bucking the system. I made plans to nurse Philip at home.

Suddenly, there was action, more talkfests, and gentle advice."A hospital was better equipped to deal with palliative care." Who says so? Now they were listening. The healthcare workers prepared a schedule and so began a long and difficult journey.

It wasn't easy to remove Philip from the system. It was an emotional rollercoaster, waiting, searching for a sign that all would be well. Sitting by the bedside, I felt overwhelmed by my uselessness in handling this insidious disease.

The change happened suddenly. Ravaging a healthy body, an unseen predator ate away at his very being, eliminating all resistance to recovery. It became a case of misdiagnosis and delayed early treatment. Would it have altered the outcome? It remains unknown. Medical science, complex and obscure, is unable to eliminate the silent killers that invade and destroy the body.

Now, walking through the empty room, I contemplate the meaning of palliative care. What does that mean? A comfortable death, never a recovery. I railed at the system. The social worker counselled acceptance of what I could not change and suggested I speak with a chaplain. I dismissed both. Philip needed my care and loving, not empty rhetoric, no matter how well meant.

And so the days passed. Family and friends visited, the doctor and nurses called, and I filled the void. Sitting by the bed, his smile filled my heart with hope as an eternal tiredness pushed me forward to cope with his daily needs. Philip must recover; miracles occur, though not too often these days in an uncertain world.

I spent the nights in a cot beside his bed, monitoring his treatment. Philip slept fitfully throughout the day, but moments of wakefulness throughout the long night built a new relationship. We talked about the future as though it were a certainty. I reached for his hand, squeezing it, a reassuring comfort to words whispered through the darkness. I hid my sadness.

We looked back on our lives together, remembering many happy and exciting moments. Through the silence of the long nights, he reminisced. "Do you remember our trip to Italy?" Philip asked in soft words between coughing fits. I smiled through the darkness, remembering his foolish attempt to drive in a foreign country with confusing road rules. He was fearless, and I was terrified, but all was well.

"Do you remember that little shop?" he asked one night when he found the energy to speak. "Those Italian lessons were worthless; still, the washing powder worked on the dishes."

We chuckled.

I caught my breath when Philip used a pet name, simply asking for a glass of water. Leaning over his emaciated frame, I never saw the wasted body, only the young, handsome man who proposed so many years earlier. Sixty years in a few months, I wish he could have waited.

"How lucky were we." Philip's words were now an effort.

"How so, my love?" I leaned closer, laying my hand on his cheek.

"Our 50th anniversary. Such an astonishing milestone. I am thankful we took that holiday."

"It stretched the budget."

"Those mountains. It was worth it. Switzerland. We shouldn't have waited so long."

"You were too busy."

"Yes. I am sorry." A tired hand brushed away a tear.

That was nearly ten years ago. I could not mention the coming anniversary. He would know.

The days passed, filled with medical procedures, nurses, and healthcare workers sent to ease his way. But the nights were the worst, so quiet and still, until a soft voice floated through the darkness.

"I'm here, my love."

"You were so beautiful, I couldn't believe my luck."

I caught my breath and took his hand, squeezing it. I was the lucky one. I had spent so many years with a man who loved me passionately and brought an honesty to our lives that few others would have experienced. I searched his eyes, so tired and heavy under the drugs administered for his comfort. Philip was fading.

"What a journey we had." I leaned closer, laying my head on his chest, whispering gently, unwilling to disturb his rest. He wrapped an arm around my shoulders.

My memory wandered. We were so young. I ignored the sceptics. Some said it wouldn't work. But it did, and as we frequently joked, 'We got it right the first time.'

"No one understood our relationship," I whispered.

He nodded. "You were a bit of a handful. But nothing I could not manage." His smile caught in the soft light now filtering through the blinds. "I always enjoyed a challenge."

I knew that. He was easily bored. Our life was never dull, with many challenges to keep us both on our toes.

I had a career when this handsome young man, popular with my friends, cast a glance my way. I was a travel writer. We both enjoyed travelling, but together.

It was simply love at first sight, something I hadn't encountered. As our relationship progressed, there was no question he was the man who would complete my life. "Until death do us part." Often spoken but never anticipated.

Then came the first test. This gentle man, so strong and confident, shook my world when he insisted I resign from my job, or at least find something that would keep me at home. My new love could not tolerate long absences. I loved my career, but it was too much to ask.

Now, remembering the terrible row, the resulting anguish when we separated, and the inevitable reconciliation, the incident was of no consequence. There would be greater hurdles to navigate.

Philip worked for Crown Law, a talented and clever man, respected and loved by his peers, with a modesty that covered his ambition.

"Elizabeth, I need you by my side," he once said, following another argument when I resisted his suggestion to resign. "You are my greatest asset."

Yes, I thought, tied to the home, always available, a beautiful hostess, so that you can climb the corporate ladder.

My objections fell on deaf ears. A smile, a cuddle, soft words and a passionate kiss always undid me.

Then the children came: three sons and a daughter, eight grandchildren, and an expected great-grandchild. A busy life stole the years until everything changed.

"What did the doctor say?" I sipped my wine, enjoying dinner at our favourite bistro. It was a quiet place, away from the hectic surroundings frequented by his colleagues.

"I've got cancer." Blunt, always to the point, a familiar trait. "I start chemotherapy next week."

Whatever surprises he had delivered throughout our long marriage, this was a shock. "It was simply a regular checkup, wasn't it?" I fought a wave of panic.

"Yes."

"You aren't sick." I shook my head, stunned. "Get another opinion."

"The blood test was positive. I have blood cancer. The specialist believes the treatment should stop it in its tracks."

Philip had already consulted a specialist. My legs buckled. How could he be so calm? He might have said, "It is a nice day." No emotion. Philip went on eating his meal.

"The chemo for a blood cancer is somewhat different to other treatments. I have applied for a six-month leave." He raised his hand, stopping my protest. "It will be alright," he insisted.

A six-month leave turned into a year, followed by a forced resignation. The stress level was too high. It would impede his recovery—except Philip didn't recover.

So many memories. Walking around the now-empty room, I pick up one of his books. He reread the edition of the Lonely Planet travel guide so often that it threatened to disintegrate in my hands. I will repair it. We had so many retirement plans. They were now meaningless.

I struggle with despair. How can I go on without him? Philip was my life, everything that mattered to me. I love my family, but we had a special relationship. We fought, we sparred, we laughed, and we cried. None of our friends understood the depth of love endured throughout the years together. He was my friend, my confidant, my lover. For a quiet man, he had a surprisingly passionate nature.

A thought crosses my mind. I suppose the family will expect me to sell up and downsize. Not yet. I need time to work through the legal details and find a way forward. Those silly comments, made years ago, still trouble my erratic mind: "You don't like change, do you?" Prophetic, but maybe true. There is little choice in life. Change is as inevitable as day following night. But this one will be very difficult to endure.

My eyes fell on family photos grouped on his side table. Our daughter Kate organised the display to show him how much he was loved.

Smiling faces, symbols of happier times, beam at me through the sadness I struggle to conceal. I turn my head towards my favourite snapshot: a distinguished man, so handsome in his judge's regalia. That was a proud moment, a promising career cut short by an insidious disease.

The courts took him from me. The pressure of the job and the daily unpleasantness of his work were too much for such a sensitive man. He never complained, though. But I suspected he would not see the job through to retirement—long days and nights demanding his attention to legal arguments, sapped his energy.

I was right, but not for the same reasons.

"Mum, are you ready?" My memories disappear through the haze of Kate's soft voice. A gentle hand on my arm. "It is time. Everyone is waiting."

One final duty. How will I cope with such a large funeral? Too many people will want to speak to me. I won't know what to say.

I look into her eyes and see the same sadness.

"Come on, we must get through this." My daughter leads me from the room, whispering, "It is time to say goodbye."

Dale Kerferd

Trinket Exchange

I'm sorry I lost
your treasures. Trinkets
handed down the generations
to reside in my care.

I am the last
of the matriarchal line,
an inheriting curator
of crockery, linen, and nicknacks.

Then I moved. I am moved
from a residence museum
to a subsistence room.

Those cherished artefacts
no longer revealed behind cupboard door,
in dresser drawer, or on mantlepiece.

My age-journey dictated
what was kept. The white China vase,
crystal rabbit, and cameo brooch
haunt my nightly repose.

The gift of lace and linen,
to the dressmaker, a faint redemption.
Now, watching Antiques Roadshow
is a memory lane guilt trip.

Kathleen Knight

A Dinosaur Called Therosorus

"Is my little princess already sleeping?" Tom asked.

"Yes! Isabella and Bonny are snuggled up together. I'm amazed that puppies can snore!" I replied cheerfully as I prepared tea and settled beside my husband, my mind bustling with thoughts.

"What's on your mind, my love?" Tom gently inquired.

"I can't help but wonder if Isabella will remember us as the years go by. How will she understand why she is living with us and not her biological parents?"

"Hey, no need to worry! We're young at heart; age is just a number," Tom said with a smile.

"I want Isabella to connect with our cultural beliefs. Keeping those memories alive is vital to fostering a strong spiritual bond with us. Understanding our Croatian heritage will enrich her life," I said, feeling passionate about it.

"It's easy! Isabella can explore our ancestry online. Keep sharing those amazing stories with her; one day, she'll piece everything together as she grows!" Tom encouraged with enthusiasm.

"Stories may fade over time, but the written word endures. I should write a memoir. I've encountered many amazing grandparents like us who serve as the primary caregivers for their grandchildren. Their valuable contributions are overlooked, unfortunately. Youth shines a spotlight in modern society while grandparents can be easily sidelined," I worried.

Tom sipped his tea and said, "Look, dear, let's be honest, writing won't be easy for you. Since English isn't your first language, you face a significant challenge. You've missed some basic grammar rules, making it a monumental task to overcome. It's like being deaf and mute during a phone call; that's how difficult it can be for you as a writer."

I was devastated. "Don't be so pessimistic; let's focus on the positive. I'll find a way to learn how to write," I said, smiling bravely.

True to my word, I joined Rockingham Writers' Centre to pursue writing. I joined a group of mostly retired seniors who wanted to write memoirs for their grandchildren.

The course participants shared stories from their youth and enjoyed watching their grandchildren grow up. The women's writing group was friendly and easy to talk to, and the room had a cozy atmosphere with lots of laughter, and the sound of teacups added to the ambience.

Teena Raffa-Mulligan, the course facilitator and an established writer, assigned us homework. I faced challenges with my English, but I persevered and wrote a short story. When it was my turn to read, I felt excited to share my stories about the granddaughter I was raising.

One grandmother commented on my story: "At our age, raising kids these days can be challenging. We grew up in a different world, but I enjoy caring for my granddaughter. She keeps me feeling young, and I wouldn't change any of it."

Teena, with an encouraging voice, guided me through her English writing journey. With steadfast support, she inspired me to submit my short story for the anthology. I enthusiastically embraced each challenge, and after Teena meticulously refined my grammar and thoughtfully edited the anthology, my words came to life in print, making my heart sing with joy.

Eager to show Tom my first masterpiece on page 81, I shared my heartfelt story, highlighting Grandcarers' crucial role in raising their grandchildren, but was disappointed when Tom didn't respond as I had hoped. I wondered if Teena felt pity for me, thinking my story needed extra help to stand out.

However, Tom's teasing only fueled my determination. "A short story isn't a big deal," he joked, "but when you write your first book, I'll read it!" His playful challenge was just the encouragement I needed to keep striving.

Suddenly, the COVID-19 pandemic interrupted everyday life and halted face-to-face learning with Teena. For me, learning online was not an option; I struggled with technology and was too scared to start something new.

After nearly two years of social isolation, I was excited to resume my creative writing courses. Teena had left her teaching job to focus on her writing career, so my next step was to enrol in a short creative writing course at the Mature Adult Learning Association (MALA).

On the first day, Rhuwina, the course facilitator, looked around the room and asked the class participants,"Why have you chosen this course?"

Some women in the class were ambitious, dreaming of writing a bestseller that could be adapted into a blockbuster movie. When it was my turn, I continued my search for a straightforward answer while the other women conversed effortlessly in fluent English.

The course focused on creative writing, completing homework assignments, and receiving constructive criticism from peers. Surprisingly, I, always known for my ability to articulate my thoughts, struggled to put pen to paper. In one of the class's practical sessions, Ms. Rhuwina asked the students to describe a rose. I thought it would be easy to write about. I began, "My garden is full of roses that provide a bountiful array of colourful blooms, though they are prickly to prune." However, that was all I could write. For the first time in my life, I felt illiterate. I now understood that writing is more complicated than telling stories verbally. That was it!

The following week, the class homework assignment was to write 200 words describing the trees in the park. I struggled to plan sentences and link my ideas into a coherent paragraph. The best I could do was jot down my thoughts: "The trees stood tall and green, some with large leaves, native plants blending in with the surroundings, with birds singing and parrots making noise."

Still haunted by my earlier mistake with the rose incident, I hesitated to read my story to the classroom, offering excuses such as being busy with my granddaughter and not having enough time.

***

Eventually, I gained enough courage to read something to my classmates. However, after listening to other students' descriptive writing, which sounded like a masterful symphony, poetry in motion, I wanted to hide under the table and disappear in shame. When the course facilitator stressed the important writing principle, 'Show, don't tell,' I felt confused and struggled to find the right words. Using bilingual dictionaries only added to my frustration, making the task even more overwhelming.

One afternoon, when I arrived home from writing, Tom asked, "What's up, dear? You look dejected."

"I struggle with descriptive writing; joining sentences into paragraphs is hard. One of my classmates joked that I might have bitten off more than I can chew. I didn't find that funny," I replied in a subdued tone.

Tom gave me one of his big bear hugs and told me, "You have an incredible talent for storytelling, but when it comes to writing, you need to develop other skills to transfer that into written words."

Seeing me upset and discouraged, he tried to lift my spirits. "How about joining an art or pottery class? You could create a beautiful flower vase and admire that elusive rose. It would bring you joy to appreciate it rather than struggle to write about it," Tom suggested.

"No way! Pottery is not for me. I must improve my English grammar and computer skills to write better. I want to write a memoir for our granddaughter to learn how we met Down-Under, fell in love, and embraced our new life in this beautiful part of the world," I insisted.

***

The following semester, I decided to enrol in another course. My teacher, Rosanne, who taught English grammar and basic computer skills, noticed that I was facing some challenges. With kindness, she suggested I revisit the basics and start with the foundational concepts of the English language from primary school. Taking this excellent advice to heart, I began exploring Isabella's primary school textbooks, which significantly improved my understanding of essential English grammar concepts.

At home, I practised on Tom's computer's outdated word processing software while my classmates relied on more advanced technology. Struggling to keep up with them, I received suggestions from some classmates to use a 'Thesaurus'. However, I was unfamiliar with this spelling aid, so quietly closed my mouth and began to ponder a vegetarian dinosaur species I had never heard of before. My critical inner voice urged me to hide and escape the scrutiny of my classmates, who were all focused on meat-eating dinosaurs.

One cozy evening at home, I happily read Isabella a delightful story about a friendly dinosaur from Teena's best-selling children's book. Each night brought a new adventure with friendly dinosaurs. While attending writing classes, I faced yet another obstacle. Using IT proved another demoralising experience for me. I couldn't help but feel inadequate as I watched my classmates effortlessly navigate their laptops, conduct online research, press many buttons, and effortlessly select the perfect words with the help of a friendly dinosaur called Thesaurus.

***

Rosanne sounded like an English literature professor, which intimidated me even more. She stressed the importance of using verbs, adjectives, adverbs, nouns, pronouns, possessive adjectives, reflexive pronouns, and conjunctions. Hearing these unfamiliar words, I initially thought these strange grammatical terms sounded more like the names of weeds in my overgrown garden rather than fundamental English grammar.

To make matters worse, I mixed up all the verbs and nouns and put them all in the wrong places while constructing sentences and connecting paragraphs.

The class exercises were demoralising. They reminded me of when I shared my embarrassment with my classmates when I didn't understand something so basic. Their laughter still echoed in my mind.

In the classroom, Rosanne noticed I was struggling with IT skills. She advised me to use the Dragon Dictaphone to record my stories and then helped me download the recordings onto the computer.

As soon as I arrived home, I eagerly shared with Tom how another dragon would help my incredible writing journey! "I just talk into the microphone, and it's like magic – my words appear on the screen! What do you think? Should I get that Dragon Dictaphone?" I asked with a bright smile, excited for this new adventure!"

"Go for it! You have nothing to lose. You're an excellent storyteller, and chatting with that dragon could lead to something fantastic!"

The next day, I happily invested three hundred dollars on Phillips' new Dragon Dictaphone, excited to capture my storytelling. However, when Tom tried transcribing my recording, he discovered that the 'Dragon' had struggled with my accent, resulting in some hilariously mixed-up words. It turned out to be a fun learning opportunity! Another charming dragon now sits proudly on the bottom shelf of my study, serving as a reminder of this delightful adventure.

Rosanne, a passionate course facilitator, supported my writing journey and enthusiastically suggested hiring a ghostwriter.

When I mentioned this to Tom, he was entirely on board with the idea. He joyfully laughed, finding the idea of ghostwriting quite amusing. "You have everything to gain," he said with a smile. "This is an option worth exploring!"

Recognising the potential of my Dragon Dictaphone, I decided to hire a ghostwriter to listen to my recordings and write my story. However, this decision turned into an expensive misadventure. Upon receiving the first two chapters, I felt disappointed; everything seemed altered and inauthentic. I wanted to preserve my unique writing style, embrace my creativity, and share my story exactly as I envisioned. Ultimately, I realised that ghostwriting was not the right path for me.

**

The following year, when a similar creative writing course was advertised, I enrolled again. This time around, reading my homework in class was slightly less painful. The new students didn't know me, which was less embarrassing. During one of the class sessions, the students were assigned to write an emotional story about sadness. I chose to share my heartfelt experience of attending the wake of my friend, who had bravely battled breast cancer. However, one of my classmates misinterpreted my story, believing the theme resembled a wedding celebration. I was again disheartened, thinking that perhaps the thoughtful facilitator from Curtin University echoed Tom by playfully suggesting that I try pottery classes instead.

When I became more comfortable with technology, I decided to try online tutorials. I sent a few chapters to editors in the eastern states, opting to remain anonymous to avoid embarrassment over my creative writing skills. Unfortunately, I encountered some unscrupulous online writing services that took advantage of me. After this experience, I preferred face-to-face learning.

I continued to practice my computer skills at home. During this time, I became friends with a resource called Thesaurus and discovered that dinosaurs were no longer so intimidating. My English grammar skills began to flourish, and I uncovered the fascinating intricacies of the language.

After years of learning, my fortunes turned positive after I joined The Society of Women Writers WA. There, I met Helen, the chairperson, a well-established, talented writer.

Helen played an instrumental role in me achieving my writing wings. We both had something in common – we were raising grandchildren. I admired Helen's tenacity. She was an exceptional grandparent who raised three grandchildren, aged three to nine, while managing a successful publishing business.

I made a point of attending all of Helen's creative writing courses. During my quest to learn how to write creatively, I met more experienced authors who inspired me to continue refining my writing. This boosted my confidence and reinforced my belief that I would complete my book. I grew more confident and realised I was mastering my creative writing skills through each experience. Embracing my progress, I looked forward to further developing my writing abilities!

After years of learning and perseverance, my dream was finally about to come true. I excitedly told Tom, "I told you I could learn to write! Helen told me that she enjoyed editing the variety of anecdotal stories about Grandcarers. The book was well written and that her company would publish it by the end of the year."

I was buzzing with excitement, jumping around like a happy wind-up doll, telling Tom, "I can't wait to touch the front cover and turn the pages; I've earned my writer's wings! Nothing can stop me now."

Tom embraced me warmly in one of his famous bear hugs, his playful spirit shining through. "Just remember, don't let this go to your head! You're no Hemingway or Tolstoy – yet! Next thing you know, you'll be announcing your Pulitzer Prize win!"

***

After dedicating eight years to mastering English grammar and refining my writing craft, in 2022 I joyfully celebrated the release of my debut book, *The Silent Heroines*. In this heartfelt story, I highlighted grandparents' struggles to raise their grandchildren, empowering them with a voice that grandcarers rightfully deserve to have. This achievement was a remarkable milestone for me, as I now felt my writing creativity had no bounds.

My enthusiasm blossomed with the release of my second book, *Tears of an Angel*, in 2024. The positive feedback from readers deeply touched me, as many found a profound connection to my storytelling. Throughout my writing journey,

I discovered a beautiful truth: writing becomes powerful when it reflects your passions and my experience is a testament to the magic that happens when passion meets purpose!

Nada Lubay

Checklist

So there I was, lying in the hospital, getting my left eye's cataract removed and replaced with a new lens. The nurse cheerfully opened my cubicle's green curtains and introduced herself: "Good morning, my name is Jenny. I will monitor your heart rate and take your blood pressure, but first I need to do a pre-op checklist and ask you a few questions. What is your name and date of birth? Are you allergic to anything, and which eye will be operated on today?"

After responding to all of the questions, she administered the eye drops, instructing Tristan, the junior male nurse, to repeat the process for the patient in cubicle Number Four every ten minutes as signalled by a timer.

"Beep, beep!" The timer went off, and Tristan cheerfully opened the curtain, saying, "Time for more eye drops. I'll be back in ten minutes for another eye drop."

The buzzer beeped again, signalling Tristan's re-entry. His comforting look and gentle smile were quite reassuring.

"You might experience some slight, temporary discomfort this time, but not for long. I'll be back after the next beep."

From my cubicle, I could hear various beeping sounds. Other patients were asked the same questions on the checklist, and it was my turn again.

Michelle, the anesthetist, walked into my cubicle. She was calm and reassuring, informing me that I'd soon be taken to the operating room. The pre-operative checklist is always the same, which includes my name, date of birth, whether I am allergic to anything, and which eye is to be operated on today. Michelle then explained the anesthetic procedure steps: "In the operating room, I will insert a needle into your arm. It's just a little prick and before you can count to ten, you will be sedated, but you will remain awake during the operation and fully conscious of your surroundings; yet you will experience no discomfort or pain." Michelle then bent down, used a black texta and marked my left eye and said, "This shows the surgeon which eye requires surgery today, but don't worry, the nurse will clean your eye after the operation."

Hearing the "Beep-Beep" sound again, Tristan opened the curtain and spoke. "Here is another eye drop solution to lubricate your left eye."

The head nurse, Linda, walked into my cubicle. She rechecked my blood pressure and pulse, then asked the usual questions.

"I answered all the questions that other nurses have repeatedly asked me – the same ones from the checklist," then I giggled, recalling something amusing.

Puzzled, Nurse Linda asked, "What is so funny? "

"Last year, my husband had a colonoscopy, and after answering a bunch of questions, he started joking around with the nurse, saying he was Elvis. When asked where he was, he said Las Vegas, and when asked what year it was now, he chuckled and belted out "2525", a song from the sixties. The junior nurse, not sure what to do, told the senior nurse that this patient is not coherent, possibly he had the onset of dementia."

"Silly man, checklists are hospital policy and not a laughing matter. The patient must understand the checklist's questions for pre-operative hospital procedures. This is vital for patient safety in all surgeries."

Beep-beep, here comes Tristan again! "This will sting a little, but it'll numb your eye before the surgery, but to distract yourself, you can watch TV until your surgery," he said.

Tristan opened the curtain on my cubicle and excitedly told me about the Blue Origin rocket launch in Texas. It's a big deal: the first flight with only women, including the pilot. He was so excited that his idol, Katy Perry, and four other famous women were heading into space.

This historic event was spellbinding, and I hadn't realised my eyes were stinging. Everyone was captivated by the Blue Origin launch, with nurses and patients tuning in to the broadcast. There was tremendous excitement as ground control entered the final stages of its pre-flight checklist and gave the launch the green light to commence the countdown – nine, eight, seven, six, five, four, three, two, one – and we have lift-off! The successful launch received immediate applause.

A nurse updated a co-worker on the historic Blue Origin trip, which included Katy Perry and other female celebrities – the first all-women spaceflight. A second nurse added, "Women are as capable as men of flying to the moon and beyond; someday, they'll even reach Mars."

Beep-Beep again. Tristan smiled as he administered the last eye drop, a soothing lubricant for the eye. He signalled the nurse, reporting that patient Number Four had received her eye drops and was ready to be wheeled to the operating room.

As I entered, the operating room resembled a Blue Origin shuttle launching against a vibrant blue sky. Overhead, the radiant lights mimicked a sunny sky, casting sunlight all over the room.

Dr Sue Yough welcomed me warmly. I had consultations with her before my surgery, and her presence during the surgery gave me a sense of safety. Once again, she calmly explained the steps and the procedure, which involved removing and replacing the lens.

She masked my face, leaving only my left eye visible. Michelle, the anesthesiologist, inserted the intravenous injection, and the bright lights temporarily blinded. During the operation procedure, I remained fully conscious. Dr Yough occasionally gave me instructions, such as moving forward, lowering my gaze, or turning my head left and right. I felt utterly relaxed and felt no discomfort at all.

"It's all done; you were a good patient. I'll see you next week to check on your recovery progress, but remember to take your eye drops for another twenty-eight days. Dr Sue Yough said as I was wheeled back to the recovery room, "We will bring you back here next month for your right eye operation."

I lost track of time in the operating theatre, but Nurse Linda explained it to me.

"The duration of your eye surgery was ten minutes, the same length as a Blue Origin flight to the stratosphere. However, the preparation takes much longer, just as Blue Origin's ground crew meticulously prepares for launch; here in the hospital, we prioritise patient safety through extensive pre-operative procedures. Rest, get dressed, and enjoy a nice sandwich and a warm cuppa. Your husband is on his way to drive you home."

While I sipped vanilla-lemon tea in the recovery room and watched TV, the same story unfolded; interviews with the Blue Origin ground crew highlighted the crucial role of safety checks. I realised how important pre-operational checklists are. I trusted the doctors and nurses, just as those brave women trusted the control room experts and the pilot's skill in ensuring Blue Origin's safe flight.

One of the crew women who flew on Blue Origin described it as an unbelievable experience. Witnessing Earth's fragility from space during the intense journey from launch to landing deepened her connection to the planet and humanity.

On the drive home with my husband, I excitedly described Blue Origin's successful launch, leaving out the details of my eye operation. I thought about how lucky those five women were.

Seeing Earth as a vast, beautiful blue sphere from high above must be incredible.

***

A few weeks later, it was time for surgery on my right eye. This time, everything felt so familiar; I recognised every sight and beeping sound. The checklist was carried out by different nurses working that day, yet I felt strangely calm and at ease following the nurses' directions. Their expertise put me at ease.

When my husband arrived to pick me up, he asked, "How was it this time?"

"Great, everything went smoothly, just like the last time." My smile reflected my confidence in the experienced ground nursing crew and the skilled surgeon who replaced the lens and restored my vision.

After twenty-eight days of using eye drops, my vision was fully restored. Best of all, I no longer need to wear glasses and feel much safer driving. I was amazed by the vibrant colours around me, which suddenly caught my eye. I don't need to go to space to appreciate the Earth's beauty from afar. Instead, I appreciate being on solid ground, taking in the breathtaking sight of my surroundings.

Nada Lubay

Switch

I'm awake, feeling the earth's clockwise rotation stop momentarily before reversing its direction, leaving me discombobulated, vertiginous. It's the twenty-first of January 2025 in Australia and the world has shifted. A switch thrown; time reversing. The progress made in the democratic world over the last century and a quarter, unravelling, a chrysalis crushed under the jackboot of a dictator.

Day one and no wars have ceased as promised. I'm unsurprised. A fragile cease-fire teeters in the Middle East, its negotiation completed before the switch. The world holds its breath.

Day ten and today seventy-eight Harmful Executive Orders and Actions have been revoked. America has reverted to a country where only two genders exist. Orders aimed at preventing discrimination based on gender diversity or sexual discrimination have been rescinded and federal funding for gender-affirming care for children under nineteen is gone. Programs facilitating diversity, equity, and inclusion in American institutions have been incinerated. Apparently, they have corrupted the government by 'replacing hard work, merit, and equality with a divisive and dangerous preferential hierarchy.' This is not just about people who are gender diverse, it is about women, people of colour, people with disabilities, that is, anyone who is not an average, white, heterosexual, American male. I belong to the half of the population that is not male. Women's equality has been hard-won and remains tenuous. America has never appointed a woman to the presidency.

Australia has only ever had one female prime minister whose misogyny speech became a battle cry for women worldwide following her appalling treatment in the Australian Parliament and the media. We still have far to go to obtain real equality and, with the clock now travelling backwards, will it at some point be decided women no longer deserve suffrage, must return to being chattels of our husbands or fathers, have no right to work in government once married, manage our own money, obtain a mortgage, retain custody of our children in the event our husband decides to divorce us (and we have no right to divorce him)? Many of these rights have been won within living memory.

March 4, and Opposition Leader Peter Dutton is following his Presidential hero, announcing the Coalition's policy to force public servants back to the office five days a week. I suspect he may change his mind on this, given its clear unpopularity. Also going under a Dutton government will be the new Right to Disconnect laws. He refutes the idea that his policies will affect women more than men. If women need flexible work, they can find job-sharing arrangements. This is the same man who continually complains that the government is failing to address the cost of living, yet seems to imagine that women only require half an income.

Gone, also by the stroke of Trump's pen, are numerous orders relating to the prevention and treatment of COVID-19; access to Medicaid and cost of prescription drugs; issues supporting the environment; ensuring safe, secure and trustworthy development and use of artificial intelligence; and promoting the Arts, the Humanities, and Museum and Library Services. Are we to burn the books now or later?

America's role as defender of democracy and the 'free world' has been abdicated. The world sits aghast watching the US President and Deputy President shred the President of a democratic ally while supporting the Russian dictatorial aggressor. This is what now passes for diplomacy. He's fond of oligarchs. Apparently, he knows some very nice ones and they can buy one of his newly minted Gold Cards if they like, for five million dollars. They can come and live in the US and pay taxes and build businesses and employ people. Having evicted thousands of poor, allegedly criminal migrants, he now intends to import rich criminals instead. Does he not understand that they have become rich most likely by criminal activity? Of course, he does. They're just like him.

On the 5th of March, the President makes a speech. He's still promising to 'reclaim' the Panama Canal and take control of Greenland; an autonomous territory of Denmark. "We strongly support your right to determine your own future," he said to the people of Greenland. "If you choose, we welcome you into the United States of America."

However, despite all his promises of choice and control, he then declares, "One way or the other, we're going to get it." This is the new way of arranging the world it seems. Canada too would be welcome to join the States. Neither Canada nor Denmark seem keen to accept the invitation. Both Canada and Mexico are being slapped with tariffs due to not doing enough to stop the influx of people and Fentanyl into the United States. Had I been incorrect in thinking that border control was the responsibility of the country being entered not exited?

Strangely, the new tariffs seem to be creating difficulties and exceptions are required to stop the American economy falling into recession, such as, on car parts from Mexico, necessary to prevent General Motors facing bankruptcy. There is no research behind Trump's policies, only what he calls Common Sense. His common sense is divergent to mine and that's the problem: Common Sense, isn't common.

There's a new way of arranging the running of the country too. Nothing like putting a billionaire in charge of slashing federal government spending. Clearly, if you can run a company like Tesla you know how to run a government, right? Elon Musk is busy finding cuts in the public service – to do so he has access to the Tax Department and thereby access to the personal and financial records of individuals and companies. Now, anyone who has ever been a public servant knows that before you commence employment you require an extensive criminal history check, must sign numerous documents, declaring that you will maintain confidentiality of all government records and data, and have completed the Department's record-keeping training module. You also need to demonstrate that you are qualified for the job that you are going to do. I am certain the same applies in the US, up until now at least. Musk is not a public servant. Has he provided any of this?

One of the first cuts of Musk's chainsaw slashed the entire US aid budget, putting millions of the world's most vulnerable people at risk of dying. Apart from likely starvation, projects battling diseases against AIDS, tuberculosis, malaria, and maternal deaths in many of the world's poorest countries would end.

Fortunately, the Federal Court has put a temporary halt on this and returned the stood-down public servants to work. There has clearly been no analysis behind the move. Even if there is no concern for the people in desperate need of aid, the link between desperation and insurrection has been ignored. It's hard to control people who have nothing to lose. Either you spend money on aid or you spend it on guns. Has COVID-19 taught him nothing about how disease travels across an uninoculated world? Does he not at least want to protect his own citizens?

Trump declares he wants peace. He's going a very strange way about it. Has he learned nothing from Afghanistan, Iraq, Gaza? Speaking of which, having allowed his friend Netanyahu to turn the whole of Gaza into rubble, he's now suggesting that of course, no one can live there; they will have to be deposited on neighbouring countries while he turns the place into a Riviera for the Middle East.

By now I am despairing: can someone not please put an adult back in charge?

March 12 and Trump's promised tariffs have come into force and he hasn't exempted Australia. Maybe our claim to be their best friend is no longer valid. In that case, perhaps we should shut down their bases and send them packing. How do we know that the intelligence they are gathering isn't being shared with Moscow, Putin and Trump being so cosy? Perhaps, though, he will inadvertently save some of WA's precious jarrah forest if the tariffs cause a slump in the profitability of South 32's aluminium production. I wait anxiously to see if there might be a glimmer of positive news amidst the gloom.

March 25, Washington's most senior national security advisor, Michael Waltz, inadvertently invites a journalist into a group chat between national security officials about a plan to bomb Yemen in *Signal*, an open-source encrypted messaging service. The journalist "could not believe that the national security leadership of the United States would communicate on *Signal* about imminent war plans." And then celebrate with emojis when the bombing killed fifty-three people! Hardly a professional way to conduct top-level security business and yet none of them have even had a slap on the wrist. I don't think Australia should be sharing information with a government that doesn't take the security of information seriously. Clearly, none of these people is qualified for the job. Remember all the palaver over Hillary Clinton's use of her personal email server to conduct government business?

March 29, a terrible earthquake strikes Myanmar. At least sixteen hundred people have died in this isolated, war-torn country. Trump magnanimously announces America will send aid, despite his previous announcement about ceasing international assistance. I fear this has more to do with hegemony than compassion. China is already in there providing substantial support to a country within its sphere of influence. If there is one country that Trump fears, it's China; he needs to maintain the power balance between this emerging force and the US. He promises to send the same amount as Australia.

He's also sent his deputy, JD Vance to Greenland, urging the population to vote to join the US. A poll taken in January has already determined that the majority of Greenlanders reject this idea. There's just been an election, a four-party coalition government has been formed; solidarity is seen as being essential against Trump's pressure. Vance's comments that Denmark has not done enough to protect Greenland from the threat of Russia and China and would be safer under American protection has not been well received in Denmark. The Danish foreign minister says, "This is not how you speak to your close allies," and there are anti-American demonstrations in Copenhagen. It's not actually the Greenlanders Trump cares about, it's his airbases, an essential part of America's missile defence infrastructure, located on the shortest route for missiles fired from Russia at the United States. He'd also quite like to get his hands on its untapped mineral and oil reserves.

I am about to consider wrist slashing, when out of the corner of my eye, I notice something new happening. A pushback is emerging. The *Tesla Takedown Movement* has been born and is stretching out, not only across the United States but in more than 230 locations across the world. I first noticed vision of the burning of Tesla cars on the news and the decrease in Tesla sales, but today there are crowds outside Tesla dealerships protesting against Musk's role heading the Department of Government Efficiency (DOGE) and his attempts to demolish government spending. The protests are taking place in many of the major cities in America, even in Tesla's home state of Texas. There's an awakening among the American people that they are living in a fascist state and a desire to reverse the trajectory. Europeans have jumped on the *Takedown Tesla* wagon. In London, there are noisy protests but in Germany, they are burning the cars. People are trying to sell their Teslas or at least slapping bumper stickers on them, distancing themselves from Musk. The company's shares have slumped. He's in denial, of course, that his company is on the nose, predicting future growth. This is a man who's not a great believer in the truth, after all.

March 31 and Trump confirms concerns expressed at his threat to dismantle democracy. In an interview with NBC News, he says he is "not joking" about trying to secure a third term as president. He states "There are methods (by) which you could do it." Not according to the 22nd Amendment. Experts on the US constitution are clear; the rules, like most things in the American system of government, are complex; but basically, no, it would not be possible to do legally, but then again, does he care about the rules?

April 2 and I am finding the American political system even more astounding. I learn, that in some states of America, judges are elected directly by the people. I'm not quite sure how I feel about that, but, in this situation, it provides some interesting information about how American electors are feeling regarding the behaviour of the president and his cronies.

In an election of a judge to the Wisconsin Supreme Court, the candidate backed by Trump and Musk was soundly defeated, despite Musk spending thirty million dollars on the race, giving two separate 'prizes' of one million dollars each, to two people who signed his petition against 'activist judges' and personally engaging in the campaign. Perhaps Americans don't like this unelected man meddling in their politics and judicial system after all. In even more encouraging news, the winner is a woman.

Trump's new round of tariffs is announced. Not only enemies like China have been badly hit but his allies have been punished too. He doesn't like the way Japan and South Korea have blocked US car makers from making inroads into their automotive market and doesn't want US brands making their products in Vietnam. He is destroying friendships decades in the making, not easily repaired. Even Australia has been hit with the base ten per cent tariff, and the most impoverished nations like Cambodia have been the worst punished; they will be charged forty-nine per cent! Financial analysts predict this intervention will make everything more expensive in the US. The people are growing concerned that they may have been lied to: Trump promised them a reduction in the cost of living. Markets around the world are slumping and a recession is forecast. In typical Trump style, he is forced to back down on some of the most excessive tariffs, except, of course, the ones against China. Markets are going up and down like yoyos with all of the uncertainty. None of this is helping the American economy.

April 16. The Judiciary is expressing fury with Trump, once again. Back in March, his administration defied a Court Order preventing it from deporting hundreds of people to a prison in El Salvadore. At least one of these individuals is completely innocent and has been deported by mistake. The Judge ordered the man's return, but a week later says the US government is doing "nothing" to facilitate this. The Judge has noted that there is "probable cause to find officials in the administration in criminal contempt," as a result. Both the presidents of the US and El Salvadore insist that there is no way to bring this poor man home! Maybe he has been lost in a totally de-personalised system.

Trump has also said he would consider jailing US citizens in prisons in El Salvadore if they had committed crimes. This sounds like Guantanamo Bay on steroids. Once a citizen is held off American soil, they no longer have any of the usual rights that by law, must be accorded to them in the US.

April 17 and there are reports of Australians being held for several hours at US airports and being sent home; Customs and Border Protection have complete control over who comes in or out and can deny entry for any reason, or none at all. They may check your phone or other devices, looking through text messages, social media and emails, either themselves or using AI, which has even more chance of misinterpreting innocent messages. Remember, there are only two genders now in the US. Just an email signature with identifying pronouns might well be enough. The head coach of the Australian mixed martial arts team claimed he spent 24 hours in an American jail when immigration officials detained him for a visa 'mistake'. I have no intention of risking any such journey.

The world and the country I grew up in and made my home has changed. An adolescent Australia, cocooned between the arms of Mother England and Father America, must now stand on her own two feet and rely on developing relationships in the neighbourhood in which she belongs. Australia has led the world in many ways, not least being the strength of its democracy; the first among nations to enfranchise women and, when compulsory voting was introduced in Queensland, it was the first place in the British Empire to do so. Our population has more than doubled since we shouted "All the way with LBJ" and found ourselves enmeshed in America's disastrous war in Vietnam and later Iraq and Afghanistan. It was America, too, that caused the 2008 Financial Crisis. This current instability is just another nail in the coffin of the Australia/America relationship and perhaps it is time for a divorce.

Part Two

It is January 2028; there should be a Presidential election in the US this year but Trump says it's an unnecessary expense. He will win anyway, he announces. Obviously, he is determined to rig any election to ensure that he does. There's no way that he would win otherwise. The American people hate him. Even his friends have deserted him. By mid-2025 Elon Musk had shifted his attention back to his business interests. Tesla was on the brink of bankruptcy. Musk, not a fan of Trump's tariffs, quickly parted ways with the President. Social Media has rejected his posts, the recipients now know they are lies and the number of his beloved band of *Proud Boys* has diminished to a handful of mentally unstable individuals. The Republican Party is in crisis. They are in the hands of an eccentric, right-wing, megalomaniac who is out of control and the Republicans in the Congress are voting with the Democrats to try to modify his outlandish decrees, to little avail. American democracy is broken.

The Whitehouse is permanently encircled by Americans begging for food, sleeping in tents. They are veterans and ex-public servants and others from tariff-impacted industries who have lost their jobs; many are previously middle-class, white Americans. They have lost their health benefits and there are no unemployment payments. They are forced to beg, but with everyone suffering in the recession, few have money to spare. The tourists, previously numerous in Washington, have gone. Their own economies impacted, they're no longer able to afford to travel to the US where everything is so expensive now, nor are they prepared to risk the vagaries of the immigration system. Unvaccinated children die of preventable diseases like measles. Babies in the tents die of malnutrition.

Inside the White House, Trump is descending further into madness. He has replaced his side-kick, Musk, with his horse, reminiscent of the self-indulgent, sadistic tyrant, Roman Emperor, Caligula. Milania has called Washington's Chief Psychiatrist but her husband has refused to see him. Despite this, he has sufficient information to make a diagnosis of Narcissistic Personality Disorder, possibly exacerbated by cognitive decline due to aging, as he's now eighty-three. The doctor also completes a forensic risk assessment and concludes that the President is a high risk of exploiting his power in a way that might put the country at serious risk and should definitely not be in control of the nuclear codes. Fortunately, high-level officials in the Pentagon have oversight of these and the rules around their use. He also suggests that Milania could be at risk due to his erratic behaviour and his anger towards her over requesting the assessment. Milania takes an extended vacation in Mar-A-Lago and surrounds herself with her personal security contingent. She has been fending her husband off with her clothing accessories for years but now hats may not be enough.

It's June 2028 and finally, the people have had enough! The crowds around the White House have swollen beyond the chronically impoverished. There are now half a million people gathering outside and the number is growing by the hour. They are chanting slogans and carrying banners: Trump Out Now!; Death to the Dictator!; Jobs for Americans!; Down with Tariffs!; Reproductive Rights for All! Reinstate Medicaid!

The crowd presses against the sturdy security fencing: it starts to give way. The crowd cheers as the security guards stand aside, their guns remaining holstered as the people flood onto the forecourt. The chanting grows louder.

Trump can be seen at the window of the Oval Office, looking out at the sea of humanity approaching the house. He calls the Head of Security. There's no answer. He calls his chief of staff:

"What the Fuck is going on? Why isn't security doing anything?"

"The guards have joined the protest, sir. I told you they needed to be paid more."

"Call the Army!"

"They are there, sir. I told you to provide more aid to Veterans."

"Call the Police!"

"You laid half of them off, sir: they don't have enough resources."

"Well do something, you stupid woman!"

The Chief of Staff goes to the front door and opens it. *At least that will stop them breaking it down; they're going to come in one way or another.*

A police officer makes his way through the crowd and approaches Trump.

"The Police, at last! Do something!"

"Yes, sir." The officer takes out his handcuffs: "Donald Trump, in the name of the American People, I am arresting you for crimes against democracy."

"You can't arrest me! I'm the President!"

"Would you rather I let this mob deal with you instead? Your choice."

The crowd cheers as Trump is led away through the crowd to a waiting police car.

There will be a democratic election in America this year but America is damaged. It is never going to be great again. In the last four years, new allegiances and trading partnerships have been formed, none of which include America. While America's economy is now in a depression, the rest of the world has recovered due to the new world trade system, now headed by China.

Australia has become a significant force in the Asia Pacific Region. While the promised AUKUS submarines have never eventuated, new long-range drone technology has replaced their security monitoring function and, combined with the new Australian-made warships, they are no longer an essential part of Australia's security requirements.

The United Nations, unable to deal with Trump, expelled America and, without US interference, a two-state solution has finally been negotiated, resolving the war between Israel and Palestine and the Europeans have chased Russia out of Ukraine. The world has discovered that it can manage quite well without the USA, and Canada and Australia have acquired some quite useful American refugees. Sometimes change can yield surprising results.

Amanda Perlinski

Note: All factual information included in this story has been sourced from the Australian Broadcasting Commission Website to ensure accuracy.

More Than Meets The Eye

I became a single mother at the age of twenty-four when my husband left my then three-year-old daughter and me. We had migrated from England to South Africa the previous year, so we had no immediate family to help us. It was heartbreaking to have to leave Orla in a childcare centre while I worked but, fortunately, we lived in a boarding house in Durban, South Africa, so our meals were provided and I could spend evenings and weekends with her. There was easy access to the beach and both Orla and I made some good friends amongst the other residents. After dinner each night, when the adults had put the children to bed, we would sit in the lounge and share coffee and life stories. There was no television in South Africa at that time and this was a pleasant way to spend the evenings.

The only person who did not join us was a young man named Paul, who came home late from work each night. After eating his meal with all of us in the dining room, he would then go straight to his room. We learnt that he was an accountant and that he brought work home to complete but he did not speak about his personal life. However, Mrs Baines, who ran the boarding house, soon filled in the gaps. She told us that his wife had left him in Johannesburg, taking their young daughter, and that he was devastated. His company had sent him to Durban to help him to get on his feet again. After my own bad experience of marriage, I empathised but I was wary of men and left it to the other residents to include him in conversation.

It was only after he had been at the boarding house for several weeks that I noticed he also left early on Sundays. I remarked on his dedication to his work to one of the other couples but was told that he was a regular churchgoer and that he went to the local Catholic Church each Sunday morning. A week or so later, a priest arrived at the front door one evening and asked for Paul. I took him to Paul's room, where he stayed for an hour or more. Once again, Mrs Baines filled us in. Paul was having counselling, she told us. A difficult time.

Although a lapsed Anglican myself, I had great respect for people who practised their faith openly, and I began to feel more relaxed in Paul's company. Here was someone with a strong sense of values, someone I could trust. Importantly, Orla enjoyed his company, too, and he told me that talking to her and watching her playing with the other children helped him to deal with the loss of his own little girl.

We found we both had an interest in horses and he asked if Orla and I would go with him to the local stables so Orla could ride her first horse. I agreed and this was the first of many Saturdays spent either at the stables or at the beach. We fell in love and the three of us spent all our spare time together. We had found happiness again.

This arrangement continued for many months, until Paul told me his company wanted him to return to Johannesburg. He told me that although the Catholic Church does not allow for remarriage after divorce it does allow for the annulment of a marriage if, as in his case, the other partner has caused the break-up. I knew his religion was extremely important to him and I respected this. We therefore agreed that Orla and I would go with him to Johannesburg. Paul's parents were strict Catholics, so to show our commitment we would need to marry at the registry office when we arrived in Johannesburg. We would later apply to have our first marriages annulled and remarry in the

Catholic Church.

Orla was three years old at this time, so I sat down with her to discuss the possibility of Uncle Paul becoming her father. She agreed so quickly that I was surprised. "He said he'll buy me a baby rabbit," she said. It made me smile at that time when I understood that a deal had already been struck. Paul would make her a good father, of that I was sure.

We married and settled in Johannesburg. Paul had four brothers and sisters, and his family were well known in the church community, so family and the church became the centre of our lives. The following year, we had a child of our own, a little girl we named Ash. Orla, her baby rabbit now grown to adulthood, was delighted to have a small sister to care for.

Soon, Orla was off to school and I worked as a secretary while our Zulu nanny, Martha, looked after both children. Paul worked as an accountant for a gold mining company. We were a close-knit family. Paul was a kind and attentive husband and he spent time either reading to the girls or playing with them when he came home from work each night. When our regular church-going friends told me how lucky I was to have him, I told them they didn't have to tell me; I already knew.

I was utterly dumbstruck, therefore, when Orla, then almost ten years old, came to me in the kitchen one evening and handed me a women's magazine she had read at a friend's house.

"Daddy wouldn't do this to me, would he?" she sobbed.

I took a quick look at the article she was pointing to. It was about stepfathers who abused their stepdaughters and what to look out for. I was horrified.

"Of course he wouldn't!" I assured her. "These are bad people. Daddy isn't like that."

"How do I know?" she sobbed again.

"Come. We'll ask him," I said, and took her by the hand to our bedroom, where Paul was reading the newspaper.

"Look at this!" I gave him the article. "Poor Orla. She thinks you might be one of these sorts of men!"

His face assumed a look of horror and disgust as he read what I had handed him, then he shook his head at Orla.

"Orla, I'm your Dad. You know I would never do this!" he said, shaking his head at her. "What sort of person would do such a thing?"

"There you are!" I told her. "You have nothing to worry about!" I hugged her and told her to throw the offending magazine in the bin. She seemed reassured, and we left Paul to read his newspaper. She didn't refer to the incident again, and I put it to the back of my mind.

It was now the nineteen seventies. It was becoming more apparent that there was little future for us in South Africa, so we applied to move to Australia. Two years later, we arrived in Perth, Western Australia. The day after our arrival, Paul visited the local Catholic School. He had with him a letter from our local priest in Johannesburg. The Principal, a nun, was clearly impressed by his commitment to Catholicism. He was, as the Principal later told me, a man whose faith shone from him. She therefore set aside the 12-month waiting list, and Orla started school the following week. Later, Ash joined Orla at the same school.

Life in Australia was working out well for us, the only frustration being that we struggled financially and lived in a unit. I wanted my family to live somewhere more comfortable, so I worked harder and harder, taking on a second job which I did from home, while Paul worked longer and longer hours in the city.

The years flashed past, and Orla was now seventeen. At last, we had enough money to buy a larger house, and she and Ash could have some of the comforts I had always wanted them to have. We built a house close to Murdoch University. I arranged for an interior designer to visit the house to discuss the décor. Orla chose her own wallpaper. Ash did the same. It was a moment I treasured. At last, my family was going to live comfortably and have the holidays we had never been able to afford.

Two days later, Orla came to me in the kitchen."Mum, I'm moving out."

The world stopped for me.

"I've found an apartment. I have a job in a restaurant working in the kitchen."

Orla, the bright student who had won the top award at her school in South Africa, was going to wash dishes. The house, the lovely house I had at last managed to provide for her. I was beside myself.

"Why, Orla? Why!?"

"I have to go, Mum. I want to be independent." And she left.

Soon afterwards, Paul left, too. He had met someone else and, despite his religious convictions, he felt he must be with her. I was blindsided. My world had fallen apart.

Orla and I didn't really speak much after that. She met a media teacher and lived with him for several years. She studied. She attended university. She did her Honours. She moved to America.

Ash and I were left to deal with the situation as well as we could. She studied and went to university. After months of therapy, I then joined her at Murdoch University as a mature-age student. Ash then wanted to go to America, too, so she followed her sister there.

Orla married. I visited them all sometimes. We were on speaking terms again, but there was a distance between us. She never explained why she had left and would not discuss the subject.

Shortly after her thirtieth birthday, I received the following email:

> *"Mum, you'll be getting something in the post. Read it but don't talk to me about it. I've been to psychologists. It's all fixed and I'm fine. As I say, I don't want to talk about it. Please honour that."*

Several days later, I received the following poem:

Duplicity

> *Saintly, she saw him*
> *Loving, always caring.*
> *Priests cleansed his soul,*
> *sanctioned it whole.*
> *A husband without sin.*
>
> *Wrong, she saw him,*
> *Touching, always watching,*
> *Cleansed not his soul,*
> *fragmented, not whole.*
> *A father with sin.*

For many years, I hated myself. How could I not have known? How could I have let my child suffer? Why couldn't she tell me? Regrettably, I knew the answer to that. As she said, I thought Paul was a saint, as did everyone else. She must have been afraid of not being believed. How awful that must have been, and how lonely.

It was not until the Catholic priest, Father Joe Tran, committed suicide in Western Australia in March 2019, when he was accused of child sexual abuse, that I understood what had

162

happened and that I could, at least in part, forgive myself. It soon became obvious to me, from newspaper articles on the case, that both Orla and I and those around us had been 'groomed'. 'Paedophiles are often charming, respected and authoritative people. Let's not forget they groom their victim and even profess their love,' one person wrote online.' [1]

This term, I found, on further research, was used by psychologists to explain the way in which predators 'strategically manipulate the victim, their family and the community to hide their deviant intentions and avoid detection.' These people, mainly men but occasionally women, don't just groom their victims, 'they groom their community to view them as trustworthy and even as spiritual leaders. They endeavour to build a good reputation and to create a strong social perception of themselves as being upstanding members of the local church or community; as nice men. These offenders will come across as very helpful, talented, funny, likable, and even wise or godly.'[2]

Paul died some years ago and even if I could speak to him about this there would be no point as I am sure he would refute the allegations; however, there is no doubt in my mind now that I was groomed and that his main interest in marrying me was never our relationship, his aim was to exploit Orla. I have honoured her request and we have never spoken about it. I can only hope the psychological help she received has allowed her to move on.

I wonder now how many children suffer silently like this and if Orla's story and her beautiful poem could help in some way. And how many mothers are duped, as I was? What clues should I have picked up on? What clues should all parents and teachers look out for? What is it that could tell us that in some seemingly happy families there are fractures beneath the surface; that there is, sadly, often more there than meets the eye?

Marilyn Rainier

1. "Shock over sex-abuse claims on dead priest Father Joseph Tran", Joe Spagnolo and Lisa Thomas, The West Australian, Sun, 24 March 2019.
2. "How predatory behaviour goes undetected in congregations", Kimi Harris, CT Christianity Today, 8 June, 2018.

Duped

It was amongst half a dozen Christmas cards to arrive that day, and the last one I opened. *'To Janet & Fred,'* it read, *'With best wishes. Hope to catch up soon. Anita and Harry.'*

I read the first name twice, to be sure I couldn't interpret the signature any other way. *Anita who?* My hands shook as I turned the envelope over. No return address. No clue on the front either; the postmark was illegible.

I checked the other envelopes. Half of them had unreadable postmarks too, and one had missed the machinery entirely. Had I steamed it open instead of my usual thumb-ripping, I could have re-used the envelope – *if it hadn't already been addressed*, I chided myself.

But returning to Anita and Harry ...

Fred was in his shed when I called, "Do you know any Anita?" I yelled.

"Henrietta? Isn't that Sally's new teacher?" he called back. Sally was our granddaughter, living with us while her parents worked out their 'differences'.

"No, Anita," I yelled.

"I thought it was Henrietta."

"Not the school teacher. She's Henrietta. I said Anita. Do you know her?" My throat was getting hoarse from yelling.

"Don't think so." A buzzing noise stopped, and he appeared at the shed door. "Who were you looking for?"

I held in a sigh. "We've just received a Christmas card from Anita and Harry. I wondered if they were friends of yours."

"Never heard of them. Are you sure it's not someone from that sewing group of yours at the church hall? Aren't you always complaining you can't remember their names?"

"How many times do I have to tell you it's not *my* group? I'm one of *them*."

Fred shrugged. "Whatever."

"You're no help," I muttered as I turned away.

"What was that?" he demanded.

"Nothing," I said over my shoulder. *Bloody deaf men. Get your hearing checked.*

"I heard that!" he called as he disappeared inside his shed.

"Hearing thoughts now, are we?" I shot back.

The buzzing noise started up again, Fred's way of ending a conversation he wasn't winning.

I returned to the kitchen. Nearly time to begin preparing dinner. I was mangling vegetables when Sally bounced in from school. "Have a good day, Sally?" I asked brightly.

She murmured noncommittally and disappeared to her room. When she reappeared, I pushed a plate of home-made biscuits and a sports drink her way – since when did today's teenagers drink anything healthy like milk?

"Thanks, Nan," she said, plonking herself onto a stool. The way she sat, I thought she seemed worried about something.

"And what did you and your friends get up to today?" I said with false bonhomie, hoping to encourage more than two words from her. She'd been so moody lately, but I remembered being the same way at her age.

"Noth..." she started, stopping as she picked up the card from Anita and Harry. I'd forgotten about leaving it on the kitchen bench, intending to interrogate Fred later. "Stupid bitch!" she muttered, staring at it.

"Tell me," I coaxed. The card shook in her hand, and her cheeks went pink.

I laid down my knife and waited. Finally, she looked up and met my gaze.

The words exploded from her. "It was such a stupid idea! Bloody Kaz!" She parodied, "'Let's prank our parents,'" in what I assumed to be her friend's voice. "Sorry, Nan, Kaz wanted to hit back at her dad and persuaded us to write dumb Christmas cards to each other's parents from imaginary people."

"Ingenious," I managed lightly. "So, do you know a Harry?"

"He's her dad."

"Not so imaginary," I said. "And Anita's who? A new girlfriend?"

Sally nodded. "You were supposed to get Connie and Clive."

I smiled, imagining what Fred would make of such names.

"What?" Sally demanded. "Why are you smiling? Do you really know a Connie and Clive?"

"No, but I'm imagining how your grandfather would mishear those names."

"You're being mysterious, Nan."

"Back in the old days, the thirties, I think, there were two outlaws in America's Wild West named Bonnie and Clyde."

The back door banged and Fred appeared. "Are they remaking the movie?" he boomed.

"No, dear. Sally and I were talking about something else."

Fred grunted and helped himself to one of Sally's untouched biscuits.

Sally slid off the stool and followed her grandfather to the lounge chairs in front of the TV. "Tell me about them, Pops," she said.

I half-listened to their conversation as I resumed chopping vegetables.

***

167

That night, I lay awake listening to Fred's rhythmic breathing. The name, Anita, had stirred memories I thought long dead. Anita Kirby and Janet Barnes. We'd attended different primary schools and met on our first day at high school when our new class teacher mixed us up because we looked alike. We sat together and discovered we had other things in common, like what we liked in boys and clothes, and which subjects we were good at and which subjects we were bad at. As our friendship developed, we spent more time at each other's homes after school. I particularly liked her parents; they were kinder and more encouraging than mine. My dad was always calling me 'hopeless' or 'stupid'. In hindsight, that's perhaps an exaggeration, but it was how I felt at the time. And having a secret crush on her older brother, Gerry, was another reason to spend less time at my own home.

During our second high school year, our parents allowed us to go to the movies together. After her brother Gerry passed his driving test, we decided to meet at the theatre and sneak off to a party with him and his mates. My last clear memory was giggling in the 'Ladies' as we styled our hair the same way, shared makeup, and even swapped name bracelets to confuse Gerry's mates.

The doctors said my memory of the car accident would return one day, but it never did. My next memory was of a dim room, lying on a bed surrounded by medical equipment, and knowing my body was broken. Awareness crept in slowly, until I saw a woman slumped in a chair nearby. The memory of that sight still rattles me. After a while, a nurse came into the room and tried to persuade her to leave.

"No! I won't go until I know for certain which one she is. I can't lose both of them, I couldn't go on!" Her gut-wrenching sobs quietened as the nurse led her away.

I closed my eyes and breathed steadily while I tried to make sense of the woman's words. Feigning unconsciousness gave me time to think. I'd recognised Janet's mother. After a while, I remembered that I was wearing Janet's name bracelet. DNA testing had yet to be invented, and I guessed visual identification in my current condition was likely impossible. She'd said, *Lose both of them*. I sensed that death was involved. Did that mean Gerry was dead?

I knew I'd hit what would now be called a *sliding doors* moment. An opportunity to change the course of my life. I hated my parents as only a teenager can, but worse, my younger brother had recently begun sneaking into my room during the night. How much longer before scaring the living daylights out of me lost its novelty and he went further? I knew Janet so well; surely I could fudge any awkward moments by claiming it was a result of the accident?

The next time I opened my eyes, Janet's mother was back in the chair. I watched her until she noticed me looking at her. "Mum," I whispered.

***

It's the weirdest feeling, reading your own name on a headstone. *Anita Kirby*. I nearly let the cat out of the bag that day, but I guess Janet's parents were so desperate to have one of their offspring still breathing that I got away with it. I tried harder to behave more like Janet and, over the years, I managed to fool them all.

Even Fred. Janet had started going out with him before the accident. The previous week, he'd given her a friendship ring. I don't know what happened to it, but I do know she intended breaking up with him the following weekend; Fred had been working on the night of the accident.

I smiled at the man sleeping beside me. If I could fool Fred, I could fool anybody. I've been doing it for over forty-five years now. Sometimes I think he suspects something, although he's never voiced doubts. And I made Janet's parents' happiness complete by presenting them with three grandsons before they died. How could that not be a good thing? While no one requests a DNA test, Anita can rest in peace.

Shirley Rowland

Ghost Writer

I'm a writer. I write. *I've always wanted to write*, I remind myself as, with each keystroke, fresh pain shoots up my arms. My right thumb is somewhere past numb. *This is what you've always wanted to do*, I argue as the ideas I'm committing to screen reach their conclusion and my fingers finally stop moving.

I read the screen, looking for typos and story gaffes. Then I check the handwritten notes beside the keyboard. I nod, satisfied that I have fulfilled the brief. The crusty detective has solved the case once more.

Yet something niggles, and I re-read the final sentence:

Detective Stub Coolman breathed in the heady scent from the avenue's flowering street trees as he strolled back to his office in downtown Brown Lane.

Wrong clue. W. B. Webb's gritty detective would never notice something about nature; he's opposed to anything environmental. He would notice a blonde woman driving a red Ferrari, the clue to set the action in motion in the seventh book in the series, but never a perfume or any other smell, unless it relates to the victim or the villain. He has selective smell in that department. I'm allowing too much of my own personality to creep into the story. I've been aware of the trend, although so far my agent, or more accurately *his* agent, has not spotted any changes in authorial voice.

I delete the offending phrase, save the changes and close the document. Proofreading can wait until tomorrow.

I rise, stretch my stiff limbs, and stumble to the kitchen. Coffee, *decaf* this time, because more than anything, I need sleep. As always, my gaze fixes on the expanse of water down the slope from this isolated rural shack. *Deadend Reach*, according to the map at the public boat ramp further down the Blackwood River. Each time I stand here, I look for the body. Surely by now it would have emerged from the reeds lining the riverbank. Maybe it never will. My skin prickles with incipient sweat, reminding me how panicked I become whenever kayakers paddle past. The last time was a week ago. Nothing came of it; no police knocking on the front door.

No one ever knocks on the front door of this shack. I don't call it mine, although I've lived here for two years now, because technically it still belongs to the body in the river. Gerry Brown, the real writer behind the alias W. B. Webb and the *Coolman* detective novels.

I met Gerry twice. The first time, I was on work experience when he visited his Perth publisher. I recall a small, thin man with bad teeth. His smile was genuine, displaying yellow, broken stubs before he remembered to lower his top lip. I was fascinated by him, partly because I'd been editing his manuscript. It was an awful piece of writing, full of clichés and poor grammar, although the storyline was ingenious. My job had been to suggest the changes needed, a task I breezed through, particularly when I realised my style was similar to his. More than anything, I yearned to be a real writer, and here was one actually making his living from it. With a lot of help from me, it turned out.

The manuscript I edited became his most popular novel yet. He invited me to visit him one day, but his agent had only post office and email addresses. No one knew where Gerry really lived. Most readers did not even know W. B. Webb was an alias.

I hadn't known where he lived until I paddled into Deadend Reach one calm morning. I assumed he'd recognised me, because he emerged from this shack and waved as he started walking down the hill. I paddled towards him and watched, horrified, as he slipped and slid, landing with a splash in the water.

I changed direction as I watched him trying to stand. Although the water was shallow, the mud was deep, and the more he struggled, the deeper he sank. I nudged the bow of my paddleboard close enough for him to grasp, but instead of helping him out, the inflated vinyl board began sinking with him.

In a panic, I used my paddle to pole-vault onto the bank and safety. On firm land, I watched him and my paddleboard disappear under the water. Apart from frantic gasps for air that ended in gurgling, he vanished silently.

I don't know how long I stood like an idiot. It was shock, I assume. *Call for help*, I told myself. I'd left my mobile phone in my car while I paddled on the river, so I hoped to find a phone in his shack. But as I trudged cautiously up a slope that was steeper than it looked, another thought came to me.

He had the career I wanted, and I had the talent to step into his shoes. *Why not?* I argued with myself. *You can't help him now. Anyway, how would they retrieve his body? And what if someone else gets sucked into that mud? It must be quicksand, or something like it. How would you feel to be responsible for more than one death?*

By the time I arrived at his back door, I'd convinced myself. I found his office and searched it. Opening his laptop was simple. He was obviously a man who struggled to remember passwords, because he'd stuck a list on the shelf above his desk. It was almost too easy to take over his life and business.

Only one problem: I'm now trapped in the drudgery of churning out a novel a year forever. No one warned me it would be so hard on both my mind and my body. Gerry had notes for several, listing the research required, but then I'll be on my own. I'm forty thousand words behind schedule on the next novel, and the current manuscript was due last week. I've never worked so hard for so little reward.

Shirley Rowland

Song of Age

Growing older is surely a curse
I hobble on, creak and groan all day
What I thought was bad is getting worse
The aches in my joints won't go away
Block my ears as you launch into verse
Relating your woes, having *your* say

The pain in your joints is worse, you say
Constant harassment from gods you curse
Irritation that won't go away
Popping those pills is making you worse
Wrinkling your image more, each sad day
Trying to force age into reverse

Suffering through your mis'r'ble verse
Consider the cure, I meanly say
Alternative to your endless curse
Something to make the pain go away
To live or to die? Which one is worse?
Take it or leave it, your choice today

When we were young, we played all day
No cares or woes, our mantra in verse
Frolicking carefree, loved life I say
Unseen the hazards we soon would curse
Deceit and heartbreak snatched youth away
I say to you now, which age is worse?

Is frailty of mind or body worse?
Choosing to focus each brand new day
On physical pain or mental curse
The choice is always open, I say
Singing life's song in rhythmical verse
Darkness and sadness pushed far away

The strength of youth may have ebbed away
Each passing day could always be worse
Maturity brings me peace today
Celebrating golden age in verse
Ignore your fragile body, I say
Dismiss the threat of old age's curse

Age may be a curse, youth's gone away
I bless each day I'm not feeling worse
Shout life's song in verse, that's all I say.

Shirley Rowland

This version was Runner-Up in 2023 Bronze Quill for Poetry

With the Flick of a Switch

A flick of a switch and a room instantly glows with light ... a simple act with the aid of Western Power. But it hasn't always been that easy. Prior to the 1960s, many rural homesteads in our area relied on an engine that "pom-pommed" loudly in a small shed. This drove the 32-volt lighting plant, which brought inert electric light globes to vibrant life and transformed silent washing machines into throbbing lifesavers. Walpole townsite was fortunate to have 240-v power provided by Bunnings Sawmill from 1968 until 1971, when power was provided by the State Energy Commission, as it was then. Bunnings actually continued to operate on its own power supply until 1974.

These 32-v plants were a boon to country folk in the surrounding districts and a vast improvement on candles and lamps. However, those who haven't experienced this type of lighting can never appreciate just how wonderful it was to see the Western Power (or SEC as it was then) machines bringing the power closer and closer to each farm property. The power that made it possible to switch on a light at the precise moment it was needed, to operate a washing machine, sewing machine, vacuum cleaner, or any other power-driven appliance without having to first start the engine was indescribable. And the joy of using an electric refrigerator compared to a temperamental kerosene model with its annoying knack of belching copious quantities of black smoke from its little chimney if its flame wasn't set quite right. And of course, it made a huge difference to operating the district dairy farms.

To the uninitiated, the starting of the engine to power the 32-v motor may not seem to present a formidable problem. But the effort to swing that big flywheel on the engine past the mysterious point of compression, which set the engine humming its rhythmic "pom-pom-pom" tune, took a strong, muscular arm – usually attached to the man of the house. Whilst he was more than happy to do the job, there were often times when he chugged off on the tractor to the realms of the unknown in the back paddock, having forgotten the plea of his spouse to "please start the engine before you go". Meanwhile, she was left wringing her hands as she surveyed the mountain of washing, ironing, or some other power-driven chore. Little wonder in that situation that farm wives also developed the necessary strength to conquer that mighty flywheel and experience the wonderful feeling of achievement as the engine sprang into life!

But those days are gone – all it needs now is the flick of a switch – and the dollars to pay the electricity account!

Molly Smith

I am Woman

A conversation I overheard the other day set me thinking. One woman mentioned to another that she had just retired, and now she was no longer a nurse, she wasn't sure how to define herself. Her companion agreed – she too had recently retired early, and was having similar problems.

As I had retired from the same profession over fifteen years ago, it set me wondering just how I now define myself.

Since I was a teenager, I have backpacked (solo many times) around the world, even crossing Europe on a moped with a tent lashed to the back – can I define myself as a world traveller? I never went to either India or China, so I guess that one is out.

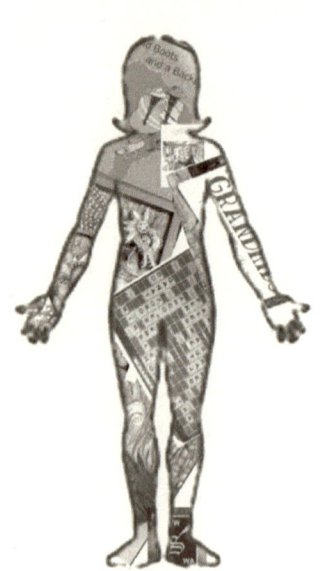

After retiring, I rediscovered a love of writing and even self-published several books. I regularly enter online writing competitions just to have a writing goal. Having joined the Society of Women Writers, I found I enjoy editing an online Writers Circle magazine and coordinating seven others. Every month, I look up different ways to design an interesting magazine cover, teaching myself from YouTube videos how to be more creative.

Can I define myself as an author – no, I feel it is only a small part of who I now am.

YouTube videos have also taught me how to Quill. I make pictures from twisted little strips of paper that are either copies of the Great Masters – Van Gogh being a favourite as his vibrant colours lend themselves to this particular art form, or copies of local landmarks. I also discovered Mixed Media Steampunk on canvas – messy, fiddly, and totally absorbing -and am currently making a large Dungeons and Dragons Steampunk picture for my daughter-in-law's next birthday, featuring a book of spells for her D&D persona, Kiki – a Druid witch. Despite having won several online and art gallery competitions for some of these pieces, can I define myself as an artist? No, once again, it is only a small part of me.

For ten years, I have been a member of an online international Scrabble League. I start each day with at least one game and have climbed near, or sometimes, to the top of the league. So, can I define myself as a Scrabble Champion? The number of times I tumbled down that ladder and had to climb back to the top again would make it a definite No!

Recently, I dragged out my old piano keyboard, and after discovering I could hardly remember where middle C was, started learning music again. Can I – or will I – ever define myself as a musician? I think my dog would beg to differ on that one!

Once a wife, a mother, a widow, I am now a grandmother and great-grandmother – though this also is not how I define myself. How can any of us define ourselves as one thing when we are capable of such diversity at different stages of our lives?

Helen Reddy summed it up perfectly – "I am Woman!"

Wendy Stackhouse

The Academy

The massive iron gates shut with an ear-shattering clang. Her tearful parents waved goodbye through the bars as she watched them dwindle into the distance. The Academy was her last chance. If they couldn't help her change, she could never go home—she had become a liability to her family.

A tear slid down her cheeks, and before she could shake it off, a deep male voice made her jump.

"I was like you when I first arrived," he said, flicking the long hair from his eyes. As a last resort, my parents abandoned me here, knowing they could no longer have me if I failed to change."

Grateful for his friendly overtures, she shyly asked him if the Academy had found a cure for him yet.

"The tutors have assured me I am almost ready to leave. My last test will be in the morning."

Despite a pang of disappointment that she would soon lose her newfound friend, hope seeped through her. If they could help change him, they must be able to help her, too, she thought.

***

A few weeks later, he was still at the Academy, having failed the final test yet again, but he would take it once more in a few days. This time, he said, with that male arrogance that she found appealing, not only would he ace the test, but he would also become one of their much-lauded star pupils.

This made her smile. Her own lessons had not been easy, but she had made a little progress and felt there was hope that one day she could return home. Initially, she dreaded being shut in the windowless room with iron sheets covering the walls, floor, and ceiling, then ordered to "Let it all out!"

At first, she struggled to obey, sobbing out her frustration instead. Many reprimands later, she had expelled a tiny breath of steam that almost knocked her over when it bounced off the metal walls. This was progress, and as the breaths became longer and hotter each time they shut her in the room, she felt the beginning of hope.

When she told her friend, he encouraged her to keep going. Despite his many failures, he would never give up, he confided. In a sudden burst of male bravado, he beat his muscled chest, making her giggle. "There is no way they will keep this beast caged up!" he said with a roar that made her jump back in mock terror. After all, despite her failure to complete her own test, she was no weakling and knew he was only trying to lift her spirits.

Over the next few months, they both found comfort in the support they gave each other whenever they managed to meet, and agreed they would never give up trying to find a cure for their problems. It was this friendship and determination that saw them both, after many setbacks, completely cured. Graduation day finally came, the same day for both of them, and they promised each other to watch their final tests.

In front of the Dean of the Academy and a select group of his star pupils, she stood alone on the dais and breathed in deeply. Then, to the accompaniment of loud cheers, she shot a searing flame skywards. Wings that, until now, had drooped behind her back, unfurled to their impressive size, causing more cheers from the assembled dignitaries. She had found her flame!

Then it was his turn—the dense hedgerows that comprised the maze parted, and he thundered forward, the horns on his head shining as he celebrated his newfound sense of direction. For the first time, he had found his way out of the labyrinth, and tail swinging behind him, he let out a bellow that reverberated around the cheering crowd.

As he approached the dais to receive his certificate, he looked up at her and gave a triumphant grin. It was unlikely they would ever cross paths again, but neither of them would forget the time they had spent together.

The Minotaur and Dragon Academy (M.A.D. for short) had once again lived up to their motto – 'Sanamus Omnia' (We cure everything!).

Wendy Stackhouse

The Woods

Dense growth concealed him as he lay flat on the ground, his shallow breathing so low it barely disturbed the birds in the branches above him. Time passed as he remained hidden, hoping they hadn't seen him changing, hoping he wouldn't have to kill them.

When he was sure it was safe to leave the darkness of the trees, he loped across the moonlit glade. A small mound of decaying leaves held the only trace of his presence, beneath which a few items of clothing lay neatly folded. Sticking up from the mound, a leafless twig with three small branches pointed upwards to the canopy of the sky.

His altered mouth twisted in a grin that resembled a toothy snarl. He remembered how last time he'd changed in the forest he couldn't find his clothes and had to return to the village naked. No one had seen him return to his cottage, but he'd vowed never to be caught in that situation again, always to place some sort of marker where he hid his clothes. Padding through the grass, he reached the edge of the glade, and leaving the bright moonlight behind, he slunk beneath the dense trees.

Time to hunt, he thought, as his salivating jaws and heightened senses picked up a familiar scent —the scent of prey. A flash of orange flew across his view, and in a few mighty bounds, he leapt onto the fleeing boar before it had time to slash him with its tusks. With one powerful snap of his elongated jaws, he broke the animal's back before tearing out its throat. How still the forest seemed when its squeals of terror and pain ended.

Settled on his haunches, he ripped chunks of warm meat

from his prize. The surrounding grass flowed with a scarlet river of blood as he devoured and crunched his way through the entire carcass.

"See, there he is," the villager cried, lifting the barrel of his gun towards the massive wolf so absorbed in his bloody meal he hadn't heard them approach. "I saw him pass the window of my cottage by the light of the moon and followed him. I have long suspected him to be the werewolf who terrorised our flocks every full moon for several years."

Behind the villager, a group of men raised their own guns and, as one, fired a volley of deathly bullets. All hit the wolf, but the one that killed him was from the first villager, who had melted down a prized silver tankard to form this special bullet. When the firing stopped, a young man, his jaws dripping with blood, lay at the feet of the vengeful men, but none wept at his demise.

"Our animals and children will be safe from now on," one man said, and they all congratulated each other on their night's work as between them they hauled the body of the dead man into a sack and dragged it back to the village.

Behind them, in the dark woods, a pair of huge yellow eyes followed their backs as they left. "You will all pay for this," the creature growled, and throwing back his massive head, he called to the rest of his pack to come and help him avenge the death of his son.

Hearing the unearthly howling, the men dropped their burden and ran, but most would never make it home, and those that did would be forever changed. With the call of the next full moon, more than half of the men of the village would leave their wives and children to join their new pack and hunt. This was the way of the woods, and of the darkness, and all the hidden things that dwelt therein.

Wendy Stackhouse

A Brother-Shaped Hole

I lost my brother when I was ten and he was eleven. It wasn't a game like Hide and Seek, where he suddenly reappeared. It was life and death, and he was gone, and my life changed forever. My parents never recovered from the loss, and I couldn't wait to escape from that ghostly house, the sad faces, haunting voices, and the brother-shaped hole. I struggled into my teens, but nothing had changed in our household, so I fled. I changed immensely and discovered boys, alcohol, and hitchhiking.

Selecting a partner of our choice usually involves planning, ticking off items from a list, and decision making, but it also includes change. It is not always easy to make changes to accommodate another person when one is used to being independent. Apart from the relationships we plan, there are some that happen when we're least expecting them. One of the most surprising connections I made was a relationship I thought wouldn't survive, but it did, and it has lasted throughout my lifetime.

Needing a change of scenery in my teens, I was thumbing a lift in Berri, South Australia, when a car slowed down and the guy in the passenger's seat wound down his window. Like most country kids, my friend Beth and I could spot West Aussie plates at a distance, so we cheered loudly when we saw the Albany rego. When the driver and his mate started talking, we soon discovered they weren't from Albany at all. They were Kiwis. Beth told them we were planning to visit New Zealand later in the year, and Rod, the driver, offered to give us his mates' phone numbers in Christchurch.

True to his word, when we saw him several days later, he gave us his list. Although he was friendly, he was not my type. With his home-knit jersey and scruffy hair, he looked like he needed a shower and a change of clothes. He was a rough diamond, whereas in my hip-hugging purple bell-bottoms and ruffled shirt, I thought I was too classy for him. I secretly hoped when I met his mates in New Zealand they would be better dressed.

Six months later, when we arrived in Christchurch, Beth and I took turns to ring the names on Rod's list. The first few guys she rang were too busy to catch up with us, but Keith, the first guy I rang, was keen to hear about Rod. Where was he? What was he doing? The last he'd heard, Rod was backpacking across the Middle East, and riding camels in Marrakesh. Had he changed much? As it had been ages since we'd last seen him, we had no idea of Rod's whereabouts, but we assumed he hadn't changed much at all. He would be the same uncouth youth that we met in South Australia.

Keith was pleased to see me again, and together we went through many changes. We got married, bought a house, and settled down in New Zealand. During the next few years, we heard that Rod was trying to survive in Afghanistan by selling his blood and/or his kidneys. He replied to Keith's letters and said he was amazed that his best mate had settled down with the classy, hitchhiking Aussie sheila he'd met in South Australia.

Our lives changed a lot during the next few years. Keith was offered a job working overseas, a great opportunity for us to save some money and start a family. We heard that Rod, meanwhile, was in Iran teaching English to pilots in the Iranian Air Force, quite a feat for someone who had trouble spelling his best friend's name on the envelope.

Keith was a product of the Catholic private school system and didn't change much over the years, whereas Rod had attended a high school in the roughest part of town and had taken the path less travelled. When I asked Keith how he and Rod happened to be such good friends, he said. 'We both have enquiring minds. We're interested in the same things. You know, metaphysics, astronomy, the universe.'

A few years later, while I was doing a degree in sociology, learning about human behaviour, how society worked, and how it could change our lives, our star-gazing friend, Rod, was studying the world first-hand in the university of hard knocks. Arrested by the Guardia Civil for stealing a motorbike in Barcelona, Rod learned how to view the world from inside a Spanish jail cell.

A few months later, Keith's widowed mother needed a partner for her Christmas work function. I suggested Rod's father, who was on his own and happened to be a good dancer. She was nervous about ringing him, but I told her, 'At your age, Nance, you've got nothing to lose.' A year later, Keith's mother married Rod's father and Keith and Rod became stepbrothers, as well as good friends.

Sadly, Keith died, and I returned to live in Perth. Rod, who'd been mining tailings at an old tin mine somewhere in the Pilbara, also ended up living in Perth. During the next few years, he supported me through my relationship breakdowns, and I supported him through his. On one occasion, his ex-wife and sister both screwed him for every cent he had. They wanted him to buy out their share in his house, so he was working three jobs to pay them back. I'd just lost my job when my son Ben had his brand-new Reeboks stolen. He was devastated, and so was I. How could I afford to replace them?

When Rod heard of his dilemma, he didn't hesitate,, but gave Ben the money to buy new shoes.

Rod's life didn't change much for the better and nor did mine, but when he was on his third marriage and I was on my second, we got on well with each other's partners and began to socialise as a foursome. He hadn't changed much and was still the rough diamond I first met, but he was a great friend. When I told him he was the closest thing I had to a brother, he was flattered.

After many years, I caught up with his sister (yes, the same one who had earlier ripped him off) and was pleasantly surprised to find she'd changed for the better. She now wanted him to be a part of her life again. I had more in common with her than I'd ever thought possible. She said Rod wanted a photo of the two of us together, his two sisters. 'Yes, he told me what you said. And I'm happy to share my brother with you.'

I'd often wondered what a deeply connected relationship would look like if I could have chosen who and what I really wanted. While some people select partners who resemble their father, others choose those who remind them of their mother. Whoever we choose, we usually end up changing ourselves to meet the needs of our partners. Despite our differences, my relationship with Rod has continued to thrive and grow stronger with time.

Over the years, I had invested a great deal of time and effort searching for the perfect relationship, trying to find a life partner or soul mate to meet my needs. After greater insight and reflection, I have changed, and I'm sure Rod has too. But it has only recently occurred to me that, after all that searching, perhaps what I really missed and needed in my life, for all those years, was someone to fill my brother-shaped hole.

Moira Yeldon

About
The Society of Women Writers WA

The Society of Women Writers was first established in Australia in Sydney in September 1925, to bring together women writers and journalists in New South Wales. Their aims were to be a social body; to promote knowledge of literature; to encourage women writers; and to strengthen the ties of interest between Australian and visiting writers.

Until the 1970s, the Society was based in Sydney, using a postal critiquing system to keep in touch. During this decade, branches were established in other Australian states and the first Federal Constitution was adopted in 1978 with an agreement that Federal responsibility be transferred from state to state every two years. Twenty years later, the decision was made to decentralise, with each state forming its own Society.

The WA branch initially operated only through correspondence groups until the first President, Ethel Webb, was appointed in 1981 and members began to meet regularly. The Society of Women Writers WA was incorporated as an autonomous body on 25 February 2000.

Contact Details
The Society of Women Writers WA
PO Box 434
125 Stirling Street
Perth Business Centre
Western Australia 6849
Tel: 0415 840 031
Email: swwofwa@gmail.com
Web: www.swwofwa.au

www.ingramcontent.com/pod-product-compliance
Lightning Source LLC
Chambersburg PA
CBHW060558190726
48283CB00003B/1068